PEOPLE
under
PRESSURE

word for **TODAY**

PEOPLE *under* PRESSURE

2 Corinthians: Strategy for stress

MICHAEL COLE

SCRIPTURE UNION
130 City Road, London EC1V 2NJ

First published 1992
by Scripture Union, 130 City Road, London EC1V 2NJ

British Library Cataloguing-in-Publication Data
A catalogue record for this book is available from the
British Library.

ISBN 0 86201 536 7

Designed by Mark Carpenter Design

Photypeset by Intype, London.
Printed and bound in Great Britain by Cox and Wyman Ltd,
Reading.

CONTENTS

INTRODUCTION

'Welcome to Corinth!'

Our plane landed at Athens Airport at 5.00 am. The temperature was already 80°Fahrenheit. My wife and I, together with two of our five children, were looking forward to a holiday on the Greek island of Poros. At last we would be able to get away from all the daily pressures!!

Ahead of us was a four hour coach journey. We had to travel from Athens, past Corinth, through the hills and across the narrow channel to Poros.

Our first stop – in what seemed to be a coach without air conditioning – was just after we had passed the Corinthian canal. We piled out of the coach into the restaurant, bought the coldest drinks possible, and sat down, our clothes sticking to us.

Despite the heat, I was thrilled to be at Corinth and in Bible lands. The actual canal had been started in the time of Emperor Nero (AD 67). The work had stopped when he died. It was not begun again until 1887, and was finished six years later. The canal is important to Corinth's trading position. Trade routes crossed North and South, East and West. Until the canal was built ships had to make the hazardous sea journey round the coast.

We were sitting about three or four miles from the site of the old city. It had been famous for its trade and for the Isthmean Games which were held there. It was also notorious because the Greek goddess, Aphrodite (the goddess of love) was worshipped there, and there were many cultic prostitutes in the city.

Greeks, Romans and Jewish people lived in the old city; they had all the pressures of any of our modern, multi-racial, multi-cultural cities.

PAUL UNDER PRESSURE

Paul, the apostle, visited Corinth three times. His first visit was a *pioneer* one that lasted eighteen months. (The story of that is found in Acts Chapter 18.) At first Paul was to preach and teach the Jews in Corinth (Acts 18:1–4), but when they rejected the message he turned to the Gentiles. It is during this first visit that Paul admits that he is feeling under pressure. He knew fear and apprehension. He faced criticism and hostility. He was rejected and abused.

Despite this hostile reception, a new young church was planted. Like other young – and not so young – churches, it had its problems. Its members polarised into various 'rival' groups. They argued about the question of spiritual gifts. They raised questions about marriage, and behaviour at the Lord's Supper. There were also some discipline problems in the church. So they asked for Paul's help in sorting all this out. In reply, Paul wrote his first letter to them, and also promised that he would visit them again personally. This second visit was to prove to be a *painful* visit, during which Paul confronted the trouble-makers. This didn't seem to solve the problem. So Paul sent a private letter to the church by Titus, one of his young associate workers. The letter had a much better reception, though there was still a good deal of criticism around. Paul then wrote his second letter – the one we are going to focus on. At the end of that letter he promised that he would make a third visit – this time it would be a *pastoral* one to encourage and help the Christians at Corinth.

You can see, then, why Paul was often under pressure himself! 2 Corinthians seems to be the letter in which Paul shows more of his real feelings and reactions than any other he wrote. In it he reveals his joy, he shows he can also be deeply hurt; he is attacked personally and has to defend himself. Paul was a man under great pressure. Three times especially he writes of being under personal pressure:

1:8 'We were under great pressure'

4:8 'We are hard pressed'

11:28 'besides everything else, I face daily the pressure of my concern for all the churches'

He was also aware of the financial pressure and constraints under which the Christians of the Macedonian churches (Philippi, Thessalonica and Berea) were living.

PRESSURES TODAY

This trip to Corinth was our first visit. Corinth, to us, meant holiday, but Corinth to Paul meant pressure, and pressures are still very much around. When Terry Wogan interviewed Princess Anne on his chat-show on

3 May 1991, she remarked, 'There are more people under pressure than ever before.' At the time of that interview the world was stunned by the cyclone destruction in Bangladesh, the famine in Ethiopia and other parts of Africa, as well as the Kurdish refugee problem in Iraq after the Gulf war.

But we don't need international crises to put us under pressure. In a paper called 'Prescription for Anxiety' (A Discussion Paper written by Dr Douglas Acres for the Churches Council on Alcohol and Drugs), it is stated that in 1979 over thirty million prescriptions for the benzodiazepine group of drugs were issued in Great Britain for the treatment of anxiety, and a further seventeen million for the problem of sleeplessness. By 1988, twenty-five million tranquilliser prescriptions a year were being handed out in Britain.

Anxiety and pressure arise from a multitude of sources. They may come from within the family or from uncertainty over jobs. They may be due to financial pressures and concerns for children, their future and ours. Pressure comes increasingly, too, simply from the pace of city life – as it must have, to some extent, in Corinth.

The massive increase in the demand for counselling, and the escape into various forms of therapy all bear witness to the growing pressure under which all of us live today. Even in Christian magazines you can find offers headlined: ' "Christian Relaxation" – Reduce the stress in your life. Protect your health. Attain inner peace and calm.'

We shall find, in this letter that Paul wrote long ago to the church at Corinth, that he speaks to people under stress and pressure. They faced the same demands to succeed, the difficulties of financial restraints, the pressures of criticism, daily routine, human weakness, and time. This letter was for them — but it is also a *word for today* to us: *people under pressure.*

1

THE PRESSURES

OF

LIFE

'Never forget that the Bible is as fresh as tomorrow's newspaper.' That advice given to George Hoffman by his former pastor has proved true in many tough places around the world. For twenty-one years George was the founding director of The Evangelical Alliance Relief Fund (TEAR Fund). His work took him to every corner of the world. He met thousands of men and women under pressure in today's world and found that God's word has a message for those struggling under the pressures.

The Bible has something important to say to each of us, about the places where we work, the troubles and pains we pass through, the opposition we face, as well as the friends we work with. So let's turn to Paul's opening words of this letter, for these are the subjects that concern him.

THE PLACE WHERE WE WORK

A friend of mine, Alan Winstanley, is the Anglican Bishop in Lima, Peru. He, his wife and family, together with the whole team of church workers, face hyper-inflation in the Peruvian economy. There are constant threats to people's lives from the Shining Path guerilla movement. Rapidly increasing numbers of people come into Lima from the surrounding areas. There are constant demands on the limited resources of the church. Added to all this, stray bullets fired by the army have been known to hit the Bishop's office door. When I asked him how he was able to remain in such work, he replied, 'It's safer to be working where God has called you, than in any beautiful spot where the Lord has *not* called you! You have to trust the Lord.'

The same was true for Paul. He was confident that he was working at the place and in the ministry that God had given him. Three times in his opening greeting to the Corinthians Paul speaks of God:

- He himself is an apostle of Christ Jesus by the will of God. He contrasts that with the claims later in the letter of the so-called 'super apostles' who were appointed by men.
- He recognises that the church at Corinth, in spite of its imperfections, belongs to God.
- He is aware of all the help – the grace and peace of God – that is available to him:

> 'Paul, an apostle of Christ Jesus by the will of God, and Timothy our brother,
> To the church of God in Corinth, together with all the saints through Achaia:
> Grace and peace to you from God our Father and the Lord Jesus Christ.'   *2 Corinthians 1:1–2*

When difficulties come there is great peace in knowing that we are working in the place and with the people that God has called us to. Equally, some pressures come when we are working in places and in jobs to which God has not called us.

One of our local church leaders, Peter, is also the financial secretary of a very large missionary society. In 1991 they faced a deficit of one million pounds in their income. This meant they had to take some very tough decisions. No one wanted to make the changes that Peter knew had to be made. But even under that pressure, he knew he was working in the job God had called him to, and that God would bring the whole Mission through safely.

There are hundreds of other people under pressure because of their jobs – teachers, businessmen, doctors, housewives, white-collar and blue-collar workers, those in social services and counselling ministries. For all of us it is vital that we know that we are doing that job 'by the will of God'.

Paul also knew that grace and peace were available. There is much in this letter about God's grace, and we shall look again at that later. The word Paul uses for 'peace' is a translation of the Hebrew word *Shalom*. It means wholeness and well-being in the midst of trouble – something found only in God and Jesus. It is not the *absence* of trouble, but help and strength in the *midst* of trouble. It is to some of those troubles that Paul now turns.

THE TROUBLES WE PASS THROUGH

More than thirty years ago our first son was stillborn. I can still recall the sense of dark isolation I felt. Whatever people tried to say to us, it didn't help, though now it is wonderful to know that he is in heaven. Though I still recall the pain of that experience, the fact that I had to pass through it has helped me to help others confronting death – whether their own or that of loved ones. I have stood where they now stand. This ability, to help others because of one's own experience of trouble, was something Paul knew, too:

> 'Praise be to the God and Father of our Lord Jesus
> Christ, the Father of compassion and the God of all
> comfort, who comforts us in all our troubles, so that
> we can comfort those in any trouble with the
> comfort we ourselves have received from God. For
> just as the sufferings of Christ flow over into our
> lives, so also through Christ our comfort overflows.
> If we are distressed, it is for your comfort and
> salvation; if we are comforted, it is for your comfort,
> which produces in you patient endurance of the
> same sufferings we suffer. And our hope for you is
> firm, because we know that just as you share in our
> sufferings, so also you share in our comfort.'
>
> *2 Corinthians 1:3–7*

Paul knew trouble! It came in the shape of persecution, the ambition to spread the gospel in places where Christ was not known, physical assaults, personal criticism, and misunderstandings. Yet he found comfort in God, and through that he was able to comfort others.

Having spoken about God three times in just the first two verses of the letter, Paul now describes God in a fatherly, comforting way, as the Father of the Lord Jesus Christ, the father of compassion, and the God of all comfort. Paul is aware that Christ's sufferings brought us the benefit of salvation. But he also knows that we will share something of Christ's sufferings as we work alongside him now. Yet as we suffer, so Christ suffers with us. So also, we can know his comfort.

That word 'comfort' or 'consolation' comes nine times (ten in the Greek!) in just five verses. That Greek word means more than someone putting their arm around our shoulder. It means to 'come alongside and help'. The Holy Spirit is also called the comforter, as he guides, strengthens and helps:

> 'Whenever we face circumstances that cause distress, there is a divine comfort for all in need. It is available at any time of pain, whether from the death of a loved one, personal failure, marital strife, family conflict, job transition, financial pressure, property loss. Whenever we hurt, God offers help.'
> (From an article by Craig Brian Larson, quoted in *Decision Magazine*, February 1991, p 34.)

There are other areas of trouble and distress that we may be facing: divorce, the anxiety of waiting for hospital X-ray results – with the haunting question, 'Is it cancer?' More people than ever before – especially men – seem to be falling victim to burnout. One such man was Myron Rush, the president of Management Training Systems in America. Yet he has written,

> 'I feel that one of the greatest benefits I derived from burn-out, was learning the true meaning of God's love. It is not conditional. It isn't based on our love for Him. It never changes no matter what we do. I knew that in theory before I burned out. But I learned it by experience when I went through burn-out.
> Another great blessing of burn-out is that you are now in a position to help others in burn-out or other difficulties they may be experiencing . . . God

helps us during our difficult times in life so we can
comfort others by reassuring them that He will help
them.'
(Myron Rush, *Burnout*. London: Scripture Press,
1989, p 152.)

Yet even though we are promised God's help and the
encouragement of others, there are still times when we
reach the end of our tether. What do we do then? Paul
wasn't afraid to admit to getting to that point.

THE END OF YOUR TETHER

'We do not want you to be uninformed, brothers,
about the hardships we suffered in the province of
Asia. We were under great pressure, far beyond our
ability to endure, so that we despaired even of life.
Indeed, in our hearts we felt the sentence of death.
But this happened that we might not rely on
ourselves but on God, who raises the dead. He has
delivered us from such a deadly peril, and he will
deliver us. On him we have set our hope that he will
continue to deliver us, as you help us by your
prayers.'   *2 Corinthians 1:8–11*

Paul readily admits that he felt he was going to die.
This was his personal feeling, rather than any sentence
passed on him by a magistrate's court of law. Yet he
derived benefit even from this: it made him rely on the
Lord who raises the dead.

Eleven years ago Reg and Mary walked out of
Guy's Hospital after Mary had been told she had breast

cancer. She was wonderfully composed. Reg admits that he was in pieces:

> We walked into the Harrard Chapel at Southwark Cathedral. How to pray? Mary brought out from her handbag the *Good News* New Testament she often carries. Literally it opened at 2 Corinthians 1:1–11. The message was very plain – we felt that the death sentence had been passed on us. But this happened so that we should rely not on ourselves, but only on God. It was one of those rare times when we were convinced that God was speaking directly. We were filled with awe and wonderful assurance. That assurance never left Mary, though I confess I wobbled a lot in the weeks that followed. But I always hung on to that passage . . . and how true and sure it was!'

Paul has to use five different expressions to get across something of the enormity of such pressure. He speaks of hardships, great pressures, being beyond his ability to endure, despairing of life, and feeling the sentence of death. Often it was Paul's friends that God used to help him through such dark times. At other times God worked through Paul's contacts, or even government officials, to bring about Paul's deliverance. So he ends by writing about God's answers to his prayers, and the people by whom those answers came.

THE FRIENDS WE NEED

> 'Then many will give thanks on our behalf for the gracious favour granted us in answer to the prayers of many.'
> *2 Corinthians 1:11*

When Paul writes about people 'helping' him and others by their prayers, he uses a Greek word which is composed of three other words: with, under, work. It is the picture of labourers shouldering a burden together, working together to get the job finished.

Paul valued his companions highly. He knew that a burden shared was a burden halved. On this occasion he writes of Timothy, his travelling and working companion at that time. Barnabas, Silas, Titus and others had fulfilled this role on other occasions. And the married couple, Priscilla and Aquila, though perhaps not quite so closely involved in Paul's work as these others, provided a home for him in Corinth where he was always met with hospitality, fellowship and support. Paul knew the value of having other people alongside to pray with, to talk things over with, and to bounce ideas off. He was even willing to receive a rebuke and correction from such friends.

Paul begins his letter thinking of the help that human partners provide. He ends the letter thinking of the fellowship that a heavenly partner, the Holy Spirit, provides. We need *both* in our lives and Christian service. Some will find that necessary human help in a marriage partner; others in a special prayer partner; others in a few good friends in whom they can confide. Paul valued highly all those people who 'laboured in prayer'. He knew their work would not go unrewarded.

It is encouraging to note how often Paul – 'the great apostle' – asked others to pray for him. We actually have more instances in the New Testament of Paul asking *others* to pray for *him*, than he is recorded as praying for other people to be saved!

A number of the businessmen in our church meet regularly on Saturday mornings to have breakfast and to pray together. They are aware of the pressures they face in their work, in the church, and that their families are under. They know the difficulties their children face at school and college. And together they help one another by their prayers, bringing their support to one another, giving practical help born out of their own experience, and calling on God to fill with his strength those who are weak and pressurised. As Paul Barnett writes, Paul's letter shows us that 'the power of God is brought to bear on man, not in man's power, but in his weakness.' (Paul Barnett, *The Message of 2 Corinthians*. Leicester: IVP, 1988, p 8).

Perhaps you know someone who is feeling the pressure at the moment. Maybe illness, bereavement, unemployment or the stresses of home or work are sapping their energy, crushing them emotionally and making them feel like giving in to despair. How can you help them to rediscover a sense of God's care and comfort, strength and direction? Here are some practical ideas:

• Don't be afraid of talking with them about how they are feeling. Assure them by your attitude, and readiness to spend time with them, that you care for them and will pray for them – and if possible, with them.

• Let them know that you won't mind what they say to you, and that you won't be shocked by anything they share with you.

• Let it be clear that you have committed yourself to that person or family for as long as need be. Show that commitment by dropping in, phoning them, and above all trying to anticipate how they may be feeling.

• Try to put yourself in their position – what must it

feel like to be in their shoes right now? Use this awareness to help you be more sensitive to their needs.

● If the pressure is caused through bereavement, plan in advance how you will help them over difficult dates, like holidays, birthdays, special anniversaries. Be aware of the fact that the second anniversary of a death is often harder to cope with than the first.

● Understand that the pain from past pressures can remain for a long time. So don't join the folk who feel that 'You should be over that hurdle now'.

● Check what practical needs a person has. Does he or she need transport to the shops or to see someone in hospital? Is help needed – especially at evening or night-time – in nursing a sick relative at home?

● Sometimes people welcome realistic and practical help in sorting out financial problems.

● What about help with babysitting – or elderly relative-sitting – so that a couple can get out once in a while?

● A cake taken round or a hot meal delivered to the family can be a wonderful encouragement to those feeling pressurised.

● If you sense that such care might become too much for you, or your own situation alters, then it is good to draw in other friends to share the caring with you.

Loving care will find many different ways – some obvious, and some very special – through which to help our friends under pressure.

2

THE PRESSURE

OF

CHANGE

People can help us cope with pressure, by their personal support and their persistent prayers. But people can also add to our pressures. There's pressure at home: the parents-in-law telling sons or daughters how to bring up their children. Gossip brings pressure at work. And even at church there's pressure: all the different groups with their different views about the hymns we sing, the style of music, the way the worship is organised, the clothes we wear, the standards we adopt and a whole host of seemingly innocent activities!

Pressure often comes most swiftly at times of change. It descends on us as we wait for exam results to arrive, for payments to be made and for urgent letters to be delivered. While we wait we become restless. We find it hard to settle to the next job.

Paul had to face three separate, and yet linked, situations of change and, on top of the stress of the unknown, his sense of pressure was increased by the way other people reacted to him. The thing that sparked off the trouble was that Paul had to change his plans – and the Corinthians criticised him for it. Then they accused him of a lack of love because he had disciplined a member of their church; and then he was forced to wait, restlessly, at Troas for his colleague, Titus, to arrive.

A businessman arrives at Heathrow early in the morning, for a flight to Brussels. A set of important meetings await him, ones he's done a lot of research for, has scheduled precisely and worked out his negotiating plans for. He's also fairly sure a successful outcome will speed up that longed-for promotion. But what happens? The flight is cancelled. His planned interviews are all missed, decisions are delayed, company plans are set back three months, all hope of promotion goes out of the window – and all because (as he put it) 'some imbecile of an aircraft engineer didn't do his job properly when he was checking the engines.'

And the pressure piles on. Already stressed by the disruption to his planned trip there's the pressure of wondering what they'll think in the office. 'He didn't try very hard, did he?' 'Bit of a no-hoper, I'd say . . . no business drive.' When he gets back there he's rude to his secretary, and when he walks in the door at home the first thing he does is kick the cat.

Paul would have sympathised. He had planned to visit the church at Corinth twice, once on his way to the Christians in Macedonia, and once on his way back. But the first visit had been so painful – as we shall see – that he felt it was wiser and kinder not to return so soon. Now they accuse him of changing his mind and of not being trustworthy.

These were *minor* changes that Paul made, but even they brought pressures in their wake. We are often faced with *major* changes – changes that come as the result of the death of a loved one; loss of friends through a move; separation or divorce; getting the sack, or gaining promotion at work. These changes always create new pressures, on top of those we already feel from the event itself.

So how should we cope with the criticism and accusations that arise if things don't turn out as we had planned and people lay the blame at our door?

CHECK YOUR CONSCIENCE

Most of us feel very guilty when we let someone down. We feel guilty because *they* are hurt and disappointed, or because we haven't done as well as *we* think we ought to have. Perhaps we need to look at our situation again and ask, 'Could I really have done anything to prevent that happening?' Often events have been totally out of our control. The businessman couldn't have made that plane fly, no matter how hard he wished it to! It does us no good to suffer from false guilt. Paul didn't; he looked carefully at his motives to see if blame really should rest on him, and this is what he concluded:

> 'Now this is our boast: Our conscience testifies that we have conducted ourselves in the world, and especially in our relations with you, in the holiness and sincerity that are from God. We have done so not according to worldly wisdom but according to God's grace. For we do not write you anything you cannot read or understand. And I hope that, as you have understood us in part, you will come to understand fully that you can boast of us just as we will boast of you in the day of the Lord Jesus.
>
> Because I was confident of this, I planned to visit you first so that you might benefit twice. I planned to visit you on my way to Macedonia and to come

back to you from Macedonia, and then to have you send me on my way to Judea. When I planned this, did I do it lightly? Or do I make my plans in a worldly manner so that in the same breath I say "Yes, yes" and "No, no"?   *2 Corinthians 1:12–17*

HOLD ON TO YOUR ORIGINAL PURPOSE

Have you ever been in the situation where you accept an invitation, but all the time your heart is saying, 'We won't go, but we'll wait till nearer the time to send our apology'? We are saying 'Yes' and 'No' at the same time! The Christians at Corinth wondered whether Paul had really intended to come and visit them. They suspected him of saying, 'Yes, I'd love to!' while thinking, 'Not on your life!' Paul denies this firmly and insists that, on the contrary, his purpose remains as steadfast as ever: he fully intends to come and see them:

> 'But as surely as God is faithful, our message to you is not "Yes" and "No". For the Son of God, Jesus Christ, who was preached among you by me and Silas and Timothy, was not "Yes" and "No", but in him it has always been "Yes". For no matter how many promises God has made, they are "Yes" in Christ. And so through him the "Amen" is spoken by us to the glory of God . . . '
> *2 Corinthians 1:18–20*

I wrote earlier about the financial secretary who had to propose cut-backs because of a deficit in his Society's income. That may have meant a change of *plan*, but it didn't imply a change of *purpose*. The financial problems didn't change the Society's aims. In fact, its magazine recently contained these words:

> 'When God sent Jesus Christ, his Son, into this world, he was in fact saying "Yes" to the world's needs, its need for salvation and community, forgiveness and fellowship, healing and health, teaching and feeding.
>
> God in Christ says YES. That, in its simplicity, is the message entrusted to the church. Through the power of the Holy Spirit we are called to make it known to all the world. But too often the church has to say NO. We can send no more missionaries. We can spare no more money. We were too busy to pray. There is nothing more we can do.
>
> Against this background the new Forward Movement of all the recognised missionary societies of our church has been launched. It challenges indifference and complacency, and recalls the church to its mission, enabling it to say YES instead of No.'
>
> (From the editorial of *Yes*, the magazine of the Church Missionary Society, September/October 1990.)

Our purposes need to be big enough to take the knocks from changes of plans and situations. Our sights need to be set on achieving the big purposes of God that he has called us into: ministering to the world's need for 'salvation and community, forgiveness and fellowship, healing and health, teaching and feeding.'

Because these purposes are God's, as well as ours, we can be sure they will be achieved. The Holy Spirit also assures us that he lives within us to strengthen and equip us for all God calls us to do – whether it turns out to be in the way and time we imagined, or not:

'Now it is God who makes both us and you stand
firm in Christ. He anointed us, set his seal of
ownership on us, and put his Spirit in our hearts as
a deposit guaranteeing what is to come.'

2 Corinthians 1:21–22

HOLD ON TO YOUR INTEGRITY

Paul was anxious that his personal integrity should not
be doubted. He realised it was vital that his word could
be trusted and his honour kept intact. And he wrote
persuasively to the Corinthians, to try to convince them
that they could trust him:

'I call God as my witness that it was in order to spare
you that I did not return to Corinth. Not that we
lord it over your faith, but we work with you for
your joy, because it is by faith you stand firm.

So I made up my mind that I would not make
another painful visit to you. For if I grieve you, who
is left to make me glad but you whom I have grieved?
I wrote as I did so that when I came I should not
be distressed by those who ought to make me rejoice.
I had confidence in all of you, that you would all
share my joy. For I wrote you out of great distress
and anguish of heart and with many tears, not to
grieve you but to let you know the depth of my love
for you.' *2 Corinthians 1:23–2:4*

Paul is aware that he is being criticised, so seeks to
defend himself. He wants to be above suspicion in all
that he does. If the Corinthians accuse him of writing
one thing, but meaning another; if they charge him with
saying one thing when present with them, and another

28

thing when he is away, then Paul will make his motives as clear as he possibly can. He wants the Corinthians to know that instead of 'lording it' over them, treating their feelings lightly, he is acting out of deep love for them.

CONFRONT RATHER THAN COMPROMISE

Paul's love for his fellow Christians meant that he would sometimes confront sin in their lives, rather than compromise with it. Professor Tasker comments: 'It takes real love to confront a difficult situation rather than side-step it.' (RVG Tasker, 2 *Corinthians*, Tyndale New Testament Commentary. Leicester: IVP, 1958, p 81.) Confrontation can be difficult, unsettling and threatening, because it tests the quality of our friendships and shows up how genuine or otherwise they are.

Which is more loving? To turn a blind eye to a teenager's excessive drinking and persistent stealing, or to confront it lovingly and show it up for what it is?

How loving is it for a Christian wife to go on putting up with the beating and violence of her husband – stemming from the violence that he had received as a young boy but now made worse by his drinking? The problem has to be confronted and his behaviour acknowledged as sin, before anything can be done to improve the situation. That is the only loving way to proceed.

So, Paul explains that not just his change of plans, but also his earlier 'painful' and confrontational visit arose out of his love. What the actual problem was, and who was the offender, we don't know. All that Paul tells us is this:

'If anyone has caused grief, he has not so much grieved me as he has grieved all of you, to some extent – not to put it too severely. The punishment inflicted on him by the majority is sufficient for him. Now instead, you ought to forgive and comfort him, so that he will not be overwhelmed by excessive sorrow. I urge you, therefore, to reaffirm your love for him. The reason I wrote you was to see if you would stand the test and be obedient in everything. If you forgive anyone, I also forgive him. And what I have forgiven – if there was anything to forgive – I have forgiven in the sight of Christ for your sake, in order that Satan might not outwit us. For we are not unaware of his schemes.'

2 Corinthians 2:5–11

We don't need to know all the details. Our human curiosity and sinful nature often rouse us to want to know about the seamy side of other people's lives! Some of our popular newspapers seem to be sold on that basis. But Paul won't parade other people's faults in public. Such an attitude prevents further sin and pressure.

Nevertheless, Paul knew the importance of discipline – for the sake of the individual Christian, the well-being of the fellowship, and the honour of the Lord. The punishment or 'penalty' for this one believer may have been a ban on coming to the Lord's Supper for some weeks. And the aim of this would have been to bring about repentance, confession and so restoration to the fellowship.

Paul is clear that the goal of confrontation is restoration, so he is anxious that the culprit is not overwhelmed by his failure and resultant discipline. He is confronting out of a motive of love, not revenge.

Paul describes Satan as wanting to 'outwit' the church. The word he uses carries the idea of defrauding a person of something that is rightly theirs. Paul doesn't want Satan to defraud the believer of his right to experience forgiveness. Nor does he want to see Satan defraud the fellowship of one of its members.

LOOK FOR NEW OPPORTUNITIES

Times of change can, of course, bring good in their wake, not simply pressure that debilitates! A change in our circumstances may be the thing God uses to steer us into new avenues of service.

'Anything for a quiet life' was not Paul's motto. We may be tempted to adopt it, but we won't find it satisfying if we do. Paul's life was far from quiet. It was demanding, and at times it was restless. He was constantly on the move, looking for new opportunities of spreading the gospel. Paul had been wondering what the next step in his Christian ministry should be. One bright idea after another had bitten the dust:

> 'Paul and his companions travelled throughout the region of Phrygia and Galatia, having been kept by the Holy Spirit from preaching the word in the province of Asia. When they came to the border of Mysia, they tried to enter Bithynia, but the Spirit of Jesus would not allow them to. So they passed by Mysia and went down to Troas. During the night Paul had a vision of a man of Macedonia standing and begging him, "Come over to Macedonia and help us." After Paul had seen the vision, we got ready at once to leave for Macedonia, concluding that God had called us to preach the gospel to them.'
>
> *Acts 16:6–10*

Now an exciting door of opportunity opened up. Instead of advancing with the gospel into the next province in Asia, God planned that Paul should move into the next *continent* of Europe, and revealed this to Paul through a vision.

Paul had learned to wait for God to reveal the next steps in his plans. Sometimes we can feel under pressure to choose quickly when opportunities arise. Maybe, like Paul, we are perplexed by meeting closed doors when we thought they were the obvious places to try. It is good to wait prayerfully for the Lord to make his plans clear to us at such times, so that any pressure we face is at least the constructive pressure of working to fulfil *God's* plan!

USE THE TIMES OF WAITING

Even with everything apparently falling into place, Paul still didn't feel peaceful! It was people again that were unsettling him – or, to be more exact, one person, Titus:

> 'Now when I went to Troas to preach the gospel of Christ and found that the Lord had opened a door for me, I still had no peace of mind, because I did not find my brother Titus there. So I said goodbye to them and went on to Macedonia.'
>
> *2 Corinthians 2:12–13*

Titus had worked with Paul. He had taken a letter to the Corinthian Church with some instructions and rebukes from the apostle, and Paul was nervously waiting to know how the letter and its contents had been received. Titus was playing a crucial role in Paul's relationship with the church at Corinth. He was to play an equally important role in the church in Crete, and one of the New Testament pastoral letters was written personally to him. Now Paul simply had to wait for Titus to come.

Paul found himself 'just waiting' at other times in his ministry, too. For example, in Acts 17:16 he was waiting at Athens for Timothy and Silas to arrive. And he decided to use the time profitably. He walked around the city, familiarising himself with it and with what the people of Athens thought, said and did. Armed with this information he was better equipped to share the gospel with them.

What do you do while waiting? Some of us find it a real pressure. Unable to settle to anything we fritter away our time and get irritable and impatient. But, like Paul, we can learn to use such times purposefully. If you find yourself with the odd stretch of time to fill, why not use it for long-term good? You could:

- Catch up on some reading – what about those Christian magazines you haven't got through yet?
- Write a letter of thanks or of encouragement to someone you know who needs it.
- Learn some verses from the Bible that are special to you.
- Pray. Ask God to make you aware of particular people or situations that need prayer at that time.
- Call on an elderly person who you know is often alone and would value a visit.
- Get to know your neighbours better.
- Do the small jobs around the house that you have always put off until you had time.

- Make that phone call to someone you have not seen for a while.
- Read through the missionary prayer letter you have put on one side.

The one thing not to do is nothing!

3

THE PRESSURE
TO
SUCCEED

Winning is what matters! We live in a world dominated by the pressure to succeed. People applaud the person who comes first, not second. A first-class degree is better than a pass-degree. The level of GCSE passes and the grades at 'A' level will govern the young person's future. The person who is intellectually bright is thought of more highly than a slow-thinker. The glamorous girl has more boyfriends than 'plain Jane'. The wealthy family who can fly off round the world seem to have more 'power' than those who just about make ends meet.

The same sort of thinking is found in the church, too. It's the large church that is thought to be the successful one, and gets more attention than the small fellowship faithfully working away in the inner city or rural village. It's the person who rises to prominence within the leadership of the church who has succeeded, rather than the man or woman who has faithfully served the Lord in the same 'back room' job for years.

Paul was aware of the pressures to succeed in his preaching. If hundreds of people weren't instantly converted, some people would want to know why! Had

Paul 'lost his touch'? But through these pressures Paul learnt that God's idea of success is often diametrically opposed to ours. For one thing, what matters is not what we *do* but who we *are*! For another, the really important thing is not what *we* do for Jesus, but what we allow *Jesus* to do in and through us. God turns the values of the world upside down. Paul had already pointed this out in his first letter to the church at Corinth:

> 'Not many of you were wise by human standards;
> not many were influential; not many were of noble
> birth. But God chose the foolish things of the world
> to shame the wise; God chose the weak things of
> the world to shame the strong. He chose the lowly
> things of this world and the despised things – and
> the things that are not – to nullify the things that
> are, so that no one may boast before him.'
>
> *1 Corinthians 1:26–29*

Perhaps not very complimentary to the Corinthians! But basic to their proper understanding of success. So how does Paul's teaching to them help us when under pressure to succeed?

HAVE REALISTIC EXPECTATIONS

Many of us come to a new task with high hopes! We're going to change everything and make 'a real difference'! Yet how often do we look back after five or ten years and wonder if we've really made any difference at all? Because we haven't succeeded in living up to our own expectations, we feel defeated failures.

When Paul came to Corinth, he came to a very

important city. Its commerce was strong and its political influence wide. It had a mixed population of Greeks, Romans and Jewish people, was a centre of learning and luxury, and was also a hotbed of vice and immorality. Paul could see that so much needed to be done! A good bit of ethical teaching for the traders and politicians, a lot of work to be done on harmonious inter-racial relationships, all those teaching posts he could take up, and the whole city needed a 'clean up morals' campaign!

Added to all this, Paul realised that the people of the city were either 'being saved' or they 'were perishing'. They were either on their way to heaven or on their way to hell. The pressure was on to preach the gospel effectively and see many people turn to Christ.

It was a daunting task, but no less so than the task that faced Rosie. She was a trained youth worker and was being appointed to a pleasant area for her work. She would have access to schools and youth clubs – but faced the pressure to succeed. Pressure from the committee who had appointed her, the churches that were paying her, the friends who were praying for her, and the colleagues who were giving their time voluntarily with her. Rosie also knew that the young people she was meeting in the schools, the clubs and on the streets did not know about Jesus or the Bible. Their spiritual understanding was virtually nil, and their church links non-existent. They had learned nothing about Christianity at home, and the RS lessons at school had been either a bit of a laugh, or a great bore.

Like Paul, Rosie had to come to terms with a hard fact: not everyone would receive her well. But she also had to understand something else: this would not be her fault – it is simply that people have the right to choose how they will respond to Christ when we present him to them. Some will accept him gladly, but others will not. So we should not be surprised to find that when we share the good news of Jesus with some people they become angry and reject what we say. They may have been brought up with the idea that there are many ways to God and are offended with the idea that Jesus is the only way. They may be sure their lives are good lives, and we offend them by talking about sin. They may be struggling with the demands of giving their lives to Christ, and we have brought up the subject again. It has always been like this. This is how Paul explains it:

> 'But thanks be to God, who always leads us in triumphal procession in Christ and through us spreads everywhere the fragrance of the knowledge of him. For we are to God the aroma of Christ among those who are being saved and those who are perishing. To the one we are the smell of death; to the other, the fragrance of life.'
>
> *2 Corinthians 2:14–16*

The apostle has in his mind a great victory procession, held in celebration of a victorious military campaign. Certain conditions had to be fulfilled for such a procession to take place in the Roman Empire. 'The Victor must have been the actual Commander-in-Chief in the field. The campaign must have been completely finished, the region pacified and the victorious troops brought home. 5000 of the enemy at least must have fallen in one engagement. A positive extension of territory must have been gained, not merely a disaster averted or an attack repelled. The victory must have been won over a foreign foe, and not in a civil war.' (William Barclay,

Letters to the Corinthians, Daily Study Bible. Edinburgh: The St Andrew Press, 1971, p 204.)

Paul has a particular battle and victory parade in mind: the battle Jesus won when, out of seeming defeat and great weakness, he died on the cross and defeated the forces of sin, evil and death. God demonstrated his victory by raising Jesus to life again on the first Easter Sunday, and now Paul sees himself united by faith with that victory, walking with Jesus as one of the conquerors. As he fights on the side of Jesus so he shares in Jesus' victory.

In a Roman victory parade the perfume of incense would rise over the procession, and the soldiers of the winning General would carry the scent of it on their bodies and clothes. To the jubilant crowd this 'scent of victory' would be like sweet perfume. But to the prisoners of war, forced to march with their captors in the victory parade, the incense would be another reminder that they were defeated and on their way to execution. In the same way, says Paul, when we have been with Jesus we carry around his 'fragrance', and we need to be realistic about people's response to this. 'Those who are being saved' will welcome it; it gives them hope and encouragement. But to those who are rejecting Christ, any reminder of him brings renewed feelings of guilt, condemnation and anger. To them he is (and we are) 'the smell of death'.

SUCCESS IS FOR PEOPLE TO SEE JESUS

In my work I am often called upon to write references for people. What can I say in their favour? How do I deal with their weak points? They know that the letter will help or hinder their job application and how other people view them. So it was with Paul. He writes:

> 'Are we beginning to commend ourselves again? Or do we need, like some people, letters of recommendation to you or from you? You yourselves are our letter, written on our hearts, known and read by everybody. You show that you are a letter from Christ, the result of our ministry, written not with ink but with the Spirit of the living God, not on tablets of stone but on tablets of human hearts.'
>
> *2 Corinthians 3:1–3*

Paul knew that the lives of his fellow Christians would be a letter of recommendation that many people would read. Some people suggest that there are five Gospel accounts of the life of Jesus: Matthew, Mark, Luke, John – and 'the Gospel according to us'!

What do people at home or work, on the train, at school or college read of the presence of Jesus from watching our lives? Whether we like it or not we are like letters about Christ; people read us to find out about him. A Sudanese national once said of the Anglican Bishop in the Sudan: 'When I see Bishop Gelsthorpe, I think I see the Lord Jesus.'

The story is told of an Indian Christian called Sadhu Sundar Singh, whose 'life letter' was a clear recommendation of Jesus. He once knocked at an Indian home and the door was opened by a little girl. She ran back into the kitchen and her mother asked her, 'Who is it?' She answered, 'I don't know, but he has such a lovely face, I think it must be Jesus!'

True success, then, is not a matter of getting *ourselves* noticed. We sometimes think: 'If I do my job really well and get promotion, that'll be a good witness!'

Well, it may be; we should of course do our jobs to the very best of our ability. But whether we get promotion or not is neither here nor there in God's view of success. What does count for success is whether people meet Jesus when they meet us:

> Not merely in the words you say,
> Not only in your deeds confessed,
> But in the most unconscious way
> Is Christ expressed.
>
> Is it a beatific smile?
> A holy light upon your brow?
> Oh no! I felt His presence
> When you laughed just now.
>
> To me, 'twas not the truth you taught,
> To you so clear, to me still dim,
> But when you came you brought
> A sense of Him.
>
> And from your eyes He beckons me,
> And from your heart His love is shed,
> Till I lose sight of you and see
> The Christ instead.

TRUST IN GOD AND HIS PLANS

It's all very well to say, 'Don't worry about being successful in "the world's" way of looking at success.' But we can feel under just as much pressure if we're told, 'What matters is that you are successful from God's point of view'! In fact, that can be an even bigger pressure because we know how hopelessly inadequate we are to the task of revealing Jesus through our lives.

More than thirty years ago I was ordained into the Anglican ministry. Everyone who is to be ordained is asked to make his or her 'ordination retreat' for the few days before the ordination service. In a sense we retreat in order to advance! Part of my three-day retreat was held in silence. We couldn't talk at meals. We had to work out how to get someone to pass the salt or marmalade! I wasn't used to this! But it was a marvellous time, and as I thought about the prospect of the ministry ahead, and of all the demands there would be on my time, skill and patience, I read these chapters in 2 Corinthians. My college principal had advised me to. 'Just let the words speak to you,' he said. And as I read repeatedly (in the *King James Version*!): 'Who is sufficient for these things?' and the ringing reply, 'Our sufficiency is of God,' God burned those words into my heart and mind.

> 'And who is equal to such a task? Unlike so many we do not peddle the word of God for profit. On the contrary, in Christ we speak before God with sincerity, like men sent from God . . .
>
> Such confidence as this is ours through Christ before God. Not that we are competent to claim anything for ourselves, but our competence comes from God. He has made us competent as ministers of a new covenant – not of the letter but of the Spirit; for the letter kills, but the Spirit gives life.'
>
> *2 Corinthians 2:16–17; 3:4–6*

There have been many times since that day when I have been under pressure to succeed, and wondered how on earth I was going to cope – a big meeting to address, a difficult committee to chair, a sensitive interview to conduct. But as I turned afresh, each time, to the Lord and his truth, he was sufficient for those things. It has even proved true in writing books!

Ian Knox is a trained lawyer but now working in full-time evangelism. He tells the story of how everything seemed to go wrong at the start of one mission:

'Picture the scene. A cold, foggy night in rural Berkshire. A twenty-two mile jam on the M4 prevents the Bishop getting to the commissioning service. Coffee has to be served at the beginning instead of the end. Can anything go right as the mission starts? Yet at the end of the service, a young man is among several who respond to Christ. "That prayer was just for me," he says. And who can counsel him? A counsellor not "on duty" that night is just leaving the church and is asked to help. He talks with the young man, who has clearly given his life to Jesus. The young man says that he has just won a music scholarship to study the cello. And who is this chance counsellor? He is the brother of the late world-renowned cellist – Jacqueline du Pre.'

Only God could work things out like that!

LIVE IN THE SPIRIT'S FREEDOM

My wife, Stephanie, and I have spent about half our ministry in the south of England, and half in the north. We have worked in great cities like Leeds, Sheffield and Manchester. For Stephanie, Manchester was probably the most difficult situation. We had moved to a very successful church and the pressure on us to succeed was great. We followed two lovely people in Michael and Myrtle Baughen. But under the pressure of trying to be

Superwife, Super-vicar's-wife and Supermum (we had five young children), Stephanie came very close to giving up the whole business of the Christian life. 'If being a Christian is a matter of "doing this," and "saying that," then I've had enough!' she thought. The pressure was getting to her.

One of the things that saved the day was a lovely Christian mum in the church. Her own story was simply that it is not what we do for Jesus that matters, but allowing the Spirit of Jesus to have his way in our lives. This is what Paul meant when he wrote, 'the letter kills, but the Spirit gives life.'

The other help was a series of taped Bible readings on Paul's letter to the Galatians, by David Pawson. The church at Galatia had fallen into the same error as we had. As Christians we were still living under the old covenant – trying to live up to particular standards and meet the demanding expectations of others – rather than enjoying freedom under the new covenant.

In these verses Paul contrasts the two. He tells us that the old covenant – great as it was – was based on a set of laws which we are constantly breaking. When we don't live up to them we are condemned as law-breakers and the death sentence is passed on us. But under the new covenant we are given Jesus' righteousness as a gift from the Spirit. Righteousness, 'being OK before God', is a gift which has to be received; it cannot be earned. Neither can anything we do wrong blow it. We are secure in God's hands – the Spirit has given us freedom from the pressure to fulfil the demands of the law.

It's like the difference between my old and new typewriter. The old one had been a twenty-first birthday present from my father. It was good. You had to hit the keys hard, but I felt comfortable and secure with it. So when I got a new, electric typewriter I was reluctant to throw the old one away. Some Christians are like that, comfortable in the familiar routine of their good deeds and church going, feeling secure in a system of earning spiritual Brownie points. They don't know how to handle something new.

For a while my new electric typewriter stood there — untried. I could understand only a bit of the instruction manual. The trouble was, the new typewriter went so fast it seemed to take over and I couldn't control it! It was only when I threw the old machine away and began to use the new, that I discovered the new life and power that was available to me.

Paul likens it to the difference between knowing someone well, personally, and knowing him only by reputation. Moses wore a veil after he had spoken face to face with God, because even the reflected glory of God's presence was too bright for the Israelites to look at! The Israelites knew God 'second hand' as it were, through Moses. But Christians don't need to rely on a second-hand knowledge of God. We can know Jesus just as Moses knew God.

It is like the bride who has come down the church aisle on her wedding day. She stands with her bridegroom and lifts back her veil. They see each other face to face. So, when we turn to the Lord, the veil that dulls our understanding of God is taken away:

> 'But whenever anyone turns to the Lord, the veil is taken away. Now the Lord is the Spirit, and where the Spirit of the Lord is, there is freedom. And we, who with unveiled faces all reflect the Lord's glory, are being transformed into his likeness with ever-

increasing glory, which comes from the Lord, who
is the Spirit.'   *2 Corinthians 3:16–18*

If we want to, we can carry on living a 'second-hand'
faith, keeping the veil on between God and ourselves.
But this is not what God wants for us. He asks us to
enter into the freedom of a full and open relationship
with him.

God intends to make this real for us each day. We
need to allow the Holy Spirit to go on filling us. In
practice this means that:

● Every day we must admit our need of the Spirit's
help, and ask Jesus to give us his Spirit.
● Sometimes we hinder the freedom of the Spirit by
our disobedience, rebellion or unbelief. We shall need
to admit this, too; turn from that attitude, ask God to
forgive us and to give us his Spirit once more.
● The Holy Spirit is like a clear, persistent voice
within, prompting us to make that 'phone call, say that
word, write that letter. As we obey his voice so we shall
rejoice to see God at work. We will discover more of
the freedom of the Spirit.
● Walking with the Spirit is like being on a journey.
Sometimes we might wander off the pathway that God
has mapped out for us. Then we need to find the path
again and follow God's instructions. As Paul put it,
'Since we live by the Spirit, let us keep in step with the
Spirit' (Galatians 5:25).

KEEP ON KEEPING ON!

For most people the pressure to succeed is not much

like running the hundred yard dash! It's much more like the long haul of running the marathon of life. Life is made up of exciting crises, and wearisome plodding. In all its ups and downs we may well be tempted to lose heart and give up. But God promises that his Spirit will go on sustaining us. He will help us to keep going:

'Therefore, since through God's mercy we have this ministry, we do not lose heart. Rather, we have renounced secret and shameful ways; we do not use deception, nor do we distort the word of God. On the contrary, by setting forth the truth plainly we commend ourselves to every man's conscience in the sight of God. And even if our gospel is veiled, it is veiled to those who are perishing. The god of this age has blinded the minds of unbelievers, so that they cannot see the light of the gospel of the glory of Christ, who is the image of God. For we do not preach ourselves, but Jesus Christ as Lord, and ourselves as your servants for Jesus' sake. For God, who said, "Let light shine out of darkness," made his light shine in our hearts to give us the light of the knowledge of the glory of God in the face of Christ.'

2 Corinthians 4:1–6

Paul never lost the sense of privilege at being caught up in God's service. He confessed that it is through the Lord's mercy that he had his apostolic ministry of preaching the gospel and caring for the church. Because of that he wouldn't lose heart and give up.

Keep on with God's truth

But Paul had pressure enough to give up! There was the temptation to misuse God's word. He could have distorted it and been deceptive about what he said, to his own advantage. Rather, he chose to tell the truth that God had given, distinctly and boldly. He could have compromised his message or he might even have curtailed his ministry.

The same temptations face the minister, preacher and Christian witness today. We might try to teach people from our own experiences rather than from the Bible (especially if our experiences make us look very spiritual!). We might choose to stress some parts of the Bible and neglect the teaching of other parts. We may fail to obey some aspect of God's teaching in our own lives so that we are powerless to teach that to others. Paul speaks of tampering with God's word. He uses a word that means to water down the wine. We can water down God's truth and try to make it more palatable: will people really go to hell if they reject Jesus? We can mix Christian teaching with philosophy from other sources. For example, there are some Christian leaders who have no problem in absorbing some New Age ideas and presenting them with their Christian teaching. We can have very strange ideas as to what mission and evangelism are in the Decade of Evangelism. A recent TV programme showed one local church using, as one means of *evangelism*, art and drama which had no reference to the Christian message!

Paul committed himself to be straightforward in sharing the teaching of the Bible. He would not be underhanded in any way, neither protecting himself from the flak that might come, nor trying to present himself as some sort of wise 'guru' who knew everything. We need to keep on witnessing to *God's* truth, as we find it in the Bible.

Keep on with prayer

Many are anxious to see their prayers answered. 'How long will it be before my son (or daughter) comes to a personal faith in Jesus?' Some Christian families seem to sail through their children's teenage years without problems. The children are committed Christians. They get involved in Christian work in their local church. They are very capable and do well at school. Everything seems to be straightforward.

Other families find it isn't as simple as that. Parents wrestle in prayer for the conversion of their family. The children aren't sure what to do when they leave school. They don't want to get involved in church because it's 'boring'. Christian parents can feel a real pressure to 'succeed' in family life. When things don't turn out well they can blame themselves and ask, 'Where did we go wrong?' The answer quite simply may be, 'You didn't go wrong anywhere. You have to realise that you are in a spiritual battle, and that Satan, the god of this world, has blinded the minds of those who don't yet believe.'

Persistent prayer – for family, friends, work colleagues, neighbours, lays the foundations for change. We need to 'keep on keeping on' in prayer.

BE AWARE OF THE OPPOSITION

Satan crops up in this letter of Paul's four or five times. He and his devilish work only increase the spiritual pressure that Christians are under. How can we counter this? What should we do? First we need to understand three things from these verses:

- *Satan is not as powerful as God.* Christians sometimes fall into the trap of thinking that because God is all-knowing, all-powerful and all present, that the same is true for Satan. The Bible's teaching is that Satan's power, presence and knowledge are limited. So take heart! Don't give up!

- *Satan attacks the mind.* The reality of this often comes through in this letter. Satan attacks the minds of unbelievers to stop them seeing the truth of who Jesus is and of his claim on them. He attacks people's minds by corrupting them, by making them lazy so that they are no longer bothered by issues of right and wrong, and by feeding them lies about Christianity and the motives of Christians. Satan also attacks the mind by confusing people's understanding of the good news. He tries to persuade them that there will be time later on to respond to Jesus. He deceives them into thinking that they will lose all their non-Christian friends if they show an interest in Jesus, or start going to church.

It is important to watch what we allow our children's minds to absorb. We *can* control some of the input. In their early days we can guide their TV watching and book reading. We can help them develop good habits of speech and thinking.

- *God can break through the darkness.* God *is* able to let his light shine in the darkness! Satan wants us to live with the curtains drawn, and to lose our faith in God's ability to change that situation. But God can throw the curtains open.

At creation God said, 'Let there be light,' and there was light. When Jesus came into the world, John described him as the light of the world coming into a world of darkness. God uses the Bible itself to speak directly to people, bringing light into dark and cloudy minds.

Thousands of people who would not otherwise catch a glimpse of Jesus do so because of the ministry of the Gideons. All around the world, groups of Gideons pray, give and work so that Bibles or New Testaments can be placed in hotel rooms, beside hospital beds or given to school children. One guest in a Bath hotel picked up the Gideon Bible in her room and became so engrossed in it that she couldn't put it down. She even took the Bible home with her! She recognised that what she found there was truth, and it gripped her mind. Her understanding was lit up. She became a Christian. Then she wrote to the local secretary of the Gideons, sent some money, explained what had happened, and asked that another Bible should be placed in room 157! Satan had tried to blind her mind, but God's truth about Jesus had broken through as she read the Bible.

So how do we go about tackling this opposition? Here are some ideas:

- Maintain a close walk with the Lord. Satan will try to prise you away from him before attacking you.
- If you know you are going to meet a particular challenge – perhaps a difficult situation at work, or a person you need to talk to – ask some friends to be praying for you at that particular time.
- Be prepared to support other Christians when they are going through a difficult time. Always be ready to offer to pray with them for God's protection and guidance. Realise that Satan will try to stop you opening your mouth – so don't be put off!

- Always be ready and willing to speak about your faith, so that you can do so the moment such an opportunity arises.
- Pray that God will make you bold, clear and courteous in conversation, and that what you say will not be misheard or misinterpreted.
- Pray to be alert to the opportunities God sends your way for speaking to non-Christians about Jesus. Have some simple Christian literature with you to give. It might be something like *Journey into life* (Kingsway), *Start a new life* (Kingsway), or *Why Jesus?* (Kingsway).

PERSEVERE THROUGH FAILURE

'But we have this treasure in jars of clay to show that this all-surpassing power is from God and not from us. We are hard pressed on every side, but not crushed; perplexed, but not in despair; persecuted, but not abandoned; struck down, but not destroyed. We always carry around in our body the death of Jesus, so that the life of Jesus may also be revealed in our body. For we who are alive are always being given over to death for Jesus' sake, so that his life may be revealed in our mortal body. So then, death is at work in us, but life is at work in you.'

2 Corinthians 4:7–12

Paul wasn't getting any younger. He was aware of his advancing years, and was growing weaker and more frail. But he did not regard his 'failing health' as a hindrance to God. Paul saw that it could be a means of blessing: the less he could rely on himself and his own abilities, the more he had to rely on God, and the more God could do through him. Just as Christians receive life through the death of Jesus, so we go on knowing life as we die to self. Our human bodies may become weaker, but our spiritual life will go on growing.

Paul compares himself to a clay jar: an ordinary, commonplace earthenware oil lamp. Such lamps could easily get dropped and broken. He felt that fragile! But the lamp held oil for the light, and that was the important thing. The light will shine out, despite the commonplace nature of the vessel. What's more, even though Paul felt as though he'd been pushed off the table and shattered into little pieces, he knew that, for the sake of the light of the gospel, God would gently gather those pieces up again and re-mould them into a stronger vessel. This is the principle of 'discovering life through death', and of increased usefulness through failure.

There *will* be times of defeat and failure in our lives – both from the world's point of view and in terms of our Christian witness. But our success, as we saw earlier, is not bound up with our own victory, but with Christ's. We are given his righteousness and the Holy Spirit to assure us that, despite our failures, we are still God's specially-loved children:

> 'It is written: "I believed; therefore I have spoken."
> With that same spirit of faith we also believe and
> therefore speak, because we know that the one who
> raised the Lord Jesus from the dead will also raise
> us with Jesus and will present us with you in his
> presence. All this is for your benefit, so that the
> grace that is reaching more and more people may
> cause thanksgiving to overflow to the glory of God.
> Therefore we do not lose heart. Though
> outwardly we are wasting away, yet inwardly we

are being renewed day by day. For our light and momentary troubles are achieving for us an eternal glory that far outweighs them all. So we fix our eyes not on what is seen, but on what is unseen. For what is seen is temporary, but what is unseen is eternal.'   *2 Corinthians 4:13–18*

Paul responded to the pressure to succeed, with the principle of faith. He speaks about 'the spirit of faith', a faith based on the fact of the resurrection. In other words, it works! Jesus is alive to prove it! What is 'sown in weakness' will be 'raised in power' (1 Corinthians 15:43).

FIX YOUR EYES ON JESUS

Despite all the pressures to give up, Paul kept on. His inspiration to do so came from Jesus: he kept his eyes firmly fixed on him.

He realised that he had been given a gracious ministry to preach the good news of Jesus to people who had never heard it. He knew that he was indwelt by the transforming Spirit of Jesus, by which he was being changed for the better, day by day. He had also glimpsed that a glorious future and hope lay ahead even for those who know that their bodies are over the hill and have seen better days. So, rather than being *driven* on by pressures on every side, Paul was *drawn* on to do God's will and to be faithful to the Lord who was still calling him.

As we are confronted day by day with the pressure to succeed in the eyes of the world, let us keep our eyes fixed on Jesus, serving him out of love rather than fear, in the power of his Spirit rather than in the merits of our own goodness, and allowing him to use all our weaknesses and failure in ways that will make us stronger to serve him. Then we can look forward to hearing the only true statement of success: 'Well done, good and faithful servant! . . . Come and share your master's happiness!' (Matthew 25:21).

4

THE PRESSURE

OF

HUMAN

WEAKNESS

If only I were young enough! If only I were clever enough! If only I were strong enough! If only I had the money! If only our marriage were better! If only I weren't feeling so ill!

I wonder how often we have thought like that? Such thoughts reveal our consciousness of human weakness. Yet we began to see in the last chapter that Paul was discovering the very important truth that God's power was available precisely to those people who realised they were weak. So we can now come to consider the pressures of human weakness that all of us face.

Mark and Julie had tried to make a success of their marriage. They had been married seven years, and had one son, James. But their relationship had gone from bad to worse. Mark blamed Julie's parents for interfering in their marriage. Julie thought the problems were due mainly to Mark's background. Both loved James but secretly believed that if he hadn't been born they would have got on better together. Julie eventually pestered Mark into going with her to see a Christian counsellor, and it helped a bit at first. But nothing really seemed to bring them closer. After a time she gave up all hope and filed for divorce.

Lucy faced a completely different problem. Peter was a wonderful husband, they had a lovely family and a stable relationship. But suddenly Peter became seriously ill and a check-up revealed a tumour. The situation was very critical. Knowing Peter might not come through the operation, Lucy felt very low and depressed.

Mark and Julie, Peter and Lucy are not exceptional. They are just two couples out of thousands who face the pressure of human weakness. Human weakness and stress were getting them down.

An article in the *Daily Mail* for 22 October 1990 stated that stress is, 'the hidden enemy of British business. It costs 328 million working days each year. Stress costs industry ten times more than all the strikes put together. The CBI (Confederation of British Industry) puts the total bill at £1.3 billion.' The stress hits women hardest, and 'a quarter of young women drink to ease the pain. The root cause of such stress might be marriage problems, bereavement or financial worries.'

One person not included in those figures was Ronald, a local church minister. He had worked in various local churches for more than twenty-five years, was well-known and well-liked, but felt 'burnt out inside'. He didn't tell anyone because he thought no-one would understand. But he had to keep pushing himself to keep going. The old inner freedom and enthusiasm seemed to have disappeared. He had already worked out how many more years he had before he could retire. He, also, was tempted to give up.

We saw, in the last chapter, that Paul faced the same temptation. He wrote twice about the pressure to lose heart, to give in to despair: 'Therefore, since through God's mercy we have this ministry, we do not lose heart' (2 Corinthians 4:1), and, 'Therefore we do not lose heart. Though outwardly we are wasting away, yet inwardly we are being renewed day by day' (2 Corinthians 4:16).

What does Paul have to say to the pressure of our own weakness? Is that an answer to it? Well, he looks at the pressure of old age or physical infirmity, and the pressure of past failures. Each of these are common experiences and each makes us feel weak and vulnerable – physically, emotionally, mentally or spiritually.

THE PRESSURE OF OLD AGE

'If only I could live life twice!' Many of us feel that if we were able to live life over again then we could make all our mistakes the first time round, and make a better job second go! Paul does, in fact, suggest that we *do* have two lives:

> 'Now we know that if the earthly tent we live in is
> destroyed, we have a building from God, an eternal
> house in heaven, not built by human hands.
> Meanwhile we groan, longing to be clothed with
> our heavenly dwelling, because when we are clothed,
> we will not be found naked. For while we are in
> this tent, we groan and are burdened, because we do
> not wish to be unclothed but to be clothed with our
> heavenly dwelling, so that what is mortal may be

swallowed up by life. Now it is God who has made us for this very purpose and has given us the Spirit as a deposit, guaranteeing what is to come.'

2 Corinthians 5:1–5

Paul is thinking about growing old, and old age brings all the problems of human weakness. Yet it can also bring hope. Paul knows that death will either decompose his body, or if the Lord returns before he dies, that his body will be transformed. Either way he will exchange the insubstantial 'tent' or his earthly body, for the durable 'house' of his eternal permanent home. The 'tent' is the suitable shelter for life here, but we'll need something different for life in eternity! George Duncan has written, 'A tent is ideal for a journey, but not for permanent residence. You can't travel in a house or dwell permanently in a tent.' (George Duncan, *Pastor and People*. Milton Keynes: Word, 1972, p 56.)

One man to whom I owe a lot was Major 'Bill Batt'. For more than twenty years he was my predecessor as the Chairman of the South American Missionary Society. Towards the end of his life, he wrote these words in a letter to Kath Clark, the Personnel Secretary of SAMS:

This earthly house, A house eternal in the heavens

You tell me I'm getting old, but that's not really so.
The house I live in may be worn and that, of course, I know.
It's been in use a good long while and weathered many a gale,
I'm therefore not surprised to find it's getting rather frail.

You tell me I'm getting old, you mix my house with me!
You're looking on the outside, that's all most folks see.

The dweller in the little house is young and bright and
  gay,
Just starting on a life that lasts through long eternal day.

The changing colour of the roof, the windows looking
  dim,
The walls a bit transparent and getting rather thin,
The foundation not so steady as once it used to be –
That's all you observe, that's not really me.

I touch the old house up a bit and make it last the night,
But soon I shall be flitting on to my home of endless light.
I'm going to live forever there, my life goes on, it's grand!
How can you say I'm getting old? You do not understand.

These few short years can't make me old, I feel I'm in my
  youth –
Eternity lies just ahead, full life and joy and truth!
We will not fret to see this house grow shabby day by
  day,
But look ahead to our new home which never will decay.

I want to be made fit to dwell in that blessed house above,
Cleansed in the precious blood of Christ and growing still
  in love.
The beauty of that glorious home no words can ever say,
'Tis hidden from these mortal eyes but kept for us some
  day.

My house is getting ready in the land beyond the sky,
Its architect and builder is my Saviour now on high.
But I rather think he's leaving the furnishing to me,
So it's treasure up in heaven I must store each day, you
  see.

Paul changes the image from a tent to that of clothes,
to reinforce his point. He pictures us as unclothed or

naked in this world, not fully equipped for life in the spiritual realm, nor yet shown off in all the glory that is ours in Christ. When our mortality is 'swallowed up', as Paul puts it, by death, then we shall be clothed with our heavenly dwelling.

Until that happens, we may find ourselves burdened with our earthly bodies. Often an older person is fed up with her arthritis, aches and pains. Frustrated that she can't get up the stairs as quickly as she used to or bend down to pick up the paper. All that may distress us and cause us to give up hope. Paul points out, though, that the best is yet to be.

The best is yet to be

But how can we be so sure? Paul gives us two reasons.

First, *heaven is what we were made for*. It's the very purpose of our existence! If life ended with death, it would be pointless and anyone who thought honestly about the meaning of their life would become incurably depressed. There *is* a heavenly home for all who love Jesus. Now that truth won't lessen the pain that Lucy feels as she sits by Peter's bedside wondering whether they will see another day together in this world. But it will give Lucy hope about the future. Death isn't the end. It will assure Peter, too, as he faces death, that he isn't going to fade away, or go into 'nothingness' or drop off the edge of existence. The earthly tent that is wearing out will be replaced with a permanent, heavenly home.

Secondly, *God has given us a guarantee*. We are assured that this is true because God has given us his Holy Spirit as a deposit, or a guarantee. The word that Paul uses is *arrabon*, a word used of an engagement ring. While it is exciting to be getting engaged and show everyone the ring, that's only a prelude to the permanence of marriage to someone you love. Paul sees death and beyond as a lasting marriage in heaven with the Lord Jesus whom he loves.

Pleasing Jesus, whether 'home' or 'away'

Because Paul knew that there were better things ahead for him, he faced the dilemma experienced by many older people, burdened with their human weakness and frailty. 'Is it better to stay around in this life, or should I pray that the Lord will come and take me home to heaven?' 'I'm ready to die, should I pray for Jesus to take me?'

> 'Therefore we are always confident and know that as long as we are at home in the body we are away from the Lord. We live by faith, not by sight. We are confident, I say, and would prefer to be away from the body and at home with the Lord. So we make it our goal to please him, whether we are at home in the body or away from it. For we must all appear before the judgment seat of Christ, that each one may receive what is due to him for the things done while in the body, whether good or bad.'
>
> *2 Corinthians 5:6–10*

Paul brings in a second 'pair' of ideas here. He writes about being at home or away. It sounds more like a football match than Christianity! Especially when Paul speaks about having a goal! Paul is actually telling us what his hope in Jesus means.

The apostle is completely honest. If he had his way, he would choose to be free from the limits of his human body, and to be in heaven with Jesus. Many elderly or ill Christians today would identify with him, those who feel they have lived long enough in this life and are more than ready to be with Jesus. They are asking the Lord to take them to himself, looking forward to what – or Who – is on the other side of the grave. However, the choice is not ultimately ours.

We do not have the right to end life. Here is a simple yet profound statement that is relevant to those who wish that euthanasia were legal. As I write this, the papers carry the story of a son and daughter set free by the Crown Courts from a charge of manslaughter. Out of love for their terminally ill mother, they had tampered with her drip-feed system in hospital so that she received, in twenty minutes, the equivalent of a 24-hour dosage of pain killer. It was their response to the groans and pleas of a desperate mum. We may understand why people want to end their lives, or those of others in great pain, but it is wrong to take life. God is the giver of life. 'In him we live and move and have our being' (Acts 17:28). We usurp the role of a loving creator when we think we have the power to end a life in this way. It is Jesus who has the keys of death and hell (Revelation 1:18), not us.

The secret is to turn our focus, with Paul, away from the negatives ('this is a really rotten situation') and onto the positives ('what can I do in this situation to please Jesus?'). Our aim or goal then will be to please him, whether we are 'at home or away'.

I wish my favourite team had that same objective! At the moment they are at the bottom of the second division, unable to win. Not so the Christian. While God leaves us in the battle, there are still victories to win. While he gives us breath, there are still ways in which we can please him.

Jesus' aim was to bend all his efforts to pleasing God. He said, 'The one who sent me is always with me; he has not left me alone, for I always do what pleases him' (John 8:29). Living out an aim like that at home and work, school and college, the church and neighbourhood, would transform life.

> 'For Christ's love compels us, because we are
> convinced that one died for all, and therefore all
> died. And he died for all, that those who live should
> no longer live for themselves but for him who died
> for them and was raised again.'
> *2 Corinthians 5:14–15*

That word translated 'compels' contains two pictures. One is the picture of a horse being reined-in by its rider. Love is the rider that reins us in from running off and going our own way. The other picture is of the river flowing between its banks. The river edges control and direct the river in the way that it should flow. Love is like the river bank directing our work and ministry.

Ronald, that local church minister, needs, I suggest, to stop for a while and take his eyes off the piles of paper on his desk, the meetings fixed in his diary, the people who think he ought to call on them, and the invitations that he would like to accept but hasn't got the energy to take. He needs to fix his eyes instead upon the limitless love of Jesus and allow that to cleanse and direct his heart, life and ministry.

Our fellowship group leaders met recently. One young leader said, 'I wonder whether I'm leading my group because the members expect me to do it or because God has called me to do it.' We need to take the time to rediscover God's calling, and to act in loving response to that, rather than in response to being 'driven' by others. Paul was called by God and so spurred on by his love for him.

But it is not only our love for God that will spur us on. An awareness of being called by him will help us to see people in a new way and gain a new love for them, too. I remember walking up the road to my church one Sunday evening. As I went past the windows people were beginning to settle down to watch the TV or to have tea. I thought to myself, 'Do I see people just as Mr and Mrs Smith at Number 23, and Mr and Mrs Jones at Number 33? Or do I see them as people whom God loves and for whom Christ died? When the second statement is true then we find that the demands of self have given way to concern for the welfare of others. With Paul we will find we have moved from 'commending ourselves' to 'no longer living for ourselves'.

Accountable for our actions

If our desire to please Jesus provides one good reason for continuing to want to live, in the face of illness or old age, another reason may come from the reminder that we will all be held accountable to God for our actions.

Paul is 'in Christ', but he is not yet 'with Christ'. He knows that death will not only bring him nearer to Christ but also nearer to judgment. He writes that we must all appear before the judgment seat of Christ, 'that each may receive what is due to him for the things done while in the body, whether good or bad.'

A verse like that raises the question: how does the truth about the judgment of God balance with the truth that when I believe in Jesus, I am justified by faith, and will not be condemned?

It is not a matter of accepting either one truth or the other, but both. The Bible often teaches two things that look at first sight to be contradictory. For example, it teaches that God is sovereign and all-powerful; it also teaches that man has free will. We are not to reject one truth and hold to the other. We are to hold both together in tension and ask why the Bible teaches both. The simple answer is because each is true. We are saved only through the death of Jesus for sinful people (justification by faith). Knowing this, we don't despair but have life and hope. But the Bible also teaches the doctrine of judgment, and we all need to know that, despite being sure of salvation, we are accountable for our actions to God, and have a responsibility to him and our neighbour.

Paul is so helpfully honest. He tells the Christians at Corinth that he is feeling anxious, hurt and vulnerable. He has shared with them the pressures of human weakness as he comes to the end of his ministry, yet he still longs to complete the task given to him. And it seems that a healthy 'fear of the Lord' played an important part in keeping him going and spurring him on:

> 'Since, then, we know what it is to fear the Lord, we try to persuade men. What we are is plain to God, and I hope it is also plain to your conscience. We are not trying to commend ourselves to you again, but are giving you an opportunity to take pride in us, so that you can answer those who take pride in what is seen rather than in what is in the heart. If we are

out of our mind, it is for the sake of God; if we are in our right mind, it is for you.'

2 Corinthians 5:11–13

To 'fear' God isn't to be frightened of him; rather, it means so to worship, reverence and be in awe of God that we are free from the temptation (and therefore the pressure) of trying to please others instead. The original word is *phobos*, from which our word 'phobia' comes. That word, as we use it now, gives us the sense of all that we fear and run away from: the dark, spiders, crowds, and so on. But when it is used in the sense of 'the fear of the Lord', it is not so much a fear of his power as a wholesome dread of displeasing him. Just as a husband will shrink from displeasing his wife, because he loves her and wants what is best for her, so a Christian, out of the fear of the Lord, wants to please him above anything else. Beside this, his fear of the effort and cost involved pales into insignificance.

THE PRESSURE OF PAST MISTAKES

Many of us would love to be able to make a fresh start in some aspect of our lives. Relationships have gone wrong; we know we have not done all we should; the pressure of failure haunts us.

As Paul writes about the great truth of the gospel, he says that its most fundamental message is all about reconciliation. It is about turning old failures into new successes:

'So from now on we regard no-one from a worldly point of view. Though we once regarded Christ in this way, we do so no longer. Therefore if anyone is in Christ, he is a new creation; the old has gone, the new has come! All this is from God, who reconciled us to himself through Christ and gave us the ministry of reconciliation: that God was reconciling the world to himself in Christ, not counting men's sins against them. And he has committed to us the message of reconciliation. We are therefore Christ's ambassadors, as though God were making his appeal through us. We implore you on Christ's behalf: Be reconciled to God. God made him who had no sin to be sin for us, so that in him we might become the righteousness of God.'

2 Corinthians 5:16–21

One Sunday on holiday, my wife and I stood in the town square of Dunkirk, France, and watched the fiftieth anniversary celebrations of the landing at Dunkirk. We saw men who had been badly wounded, and widows proudly marching in the place of their dead husbands. Out of the suffering of these people had come peace. But it was costly.

That is a principle true for nations as well as for individuals. This was brought home to me powerfully by the account of some events that took place on a previous Remembrance Sunday. In a church not far from us, a Sister of the German Evangelical Sisterhood of Mary stood up at the end of the Remembrance service to ask publicly for forgiveness for her nation's guilt in war. In turn, the vicar asked her forgiveness for the things we had done to her land – including the bombing of Darmstadt, where the sisters have their Mother-house.

What a lovely expression of the message and the

ministry of reconciliation. The old enmity and failure had been replaced by a new covenant of love in Christ.

The real wonder is that God isn't content just to patch up the failures in our lives, or even try to keep the *status quo*. He is in the business of making 'all things new.' This involves acknowledging our failures, and confessing and repenting of our sins. It means a commitment to live a new way of life.

Reconciliation is needed in many areas of life today. It is needed between husband and wife, Catholic and Protestant, Arab and Jew, black and white. Take the experience of Caesar Molebatsi. Caesar was knocked down by a car driven by a white man in the black township of Soweto near Johannesburg, at Christmas 1964. He was 15. His leg was badly broken in two places and he was bleeding profusely from multiple injuries. The driver checked he wasn't dead, draped a blanket over him and went to report the accident to the nearest police station.

Thirty-eight minutes later the police arrived. Caesar was refused admission at the nearest hospital because he was black and he had to be driven another twenty-five miles to hospital. For three weeks he lay in agony due to inadequate treatment. Gangrene was diagnosed in his leg, which then had to be amputated. He was left a deeply embittered teenager, vowing to spend the rest of his life 'driving the whites back into the sea'.

Instead, today Caesar is one of the leading evangelical spokesmen for the black community in South Africa, travelling widely, and he is chairman of 'Concerned Evangelicals' – a black-led group of 130 people which produced the challenging and outspoken document, 'Evangelical Witness in South Africa'.

The change and reconciliation in Caesar's life came about through a white Christian who kept vigil with him. For long periods this Christian sat with Caesar in his home, Caesar refusing to speak. Three years later, the breakthrough came. He went to some meetings of Youth Alive, a Christian ministry in Soweto. There he found such love and acceptance that he opened his life to God and was able to forgive his enemies.

His story illustrates for us what Paul has been writing about. The white Christian saw Caesar from a new perspective. He could see that God could make all things new. What's more, he had a new purpose – to share the message of reconciliation with Caesar. He saw that he was an ambassador to Caesar, in the place of Jesus, urging him to be reconciled to God. In turn, Caesar himself became the ambassador to black and white in South Africa. He who had been changed, now became the agent of change to others.

'Well, that's all right for him!' I wonder if that is the reaction we often give to such stories? It is all right for other people, but it will never happen for me! God doesn't answer *my* prayers like that. I shall just have to put up with life as it is, and live with my failure and inadequacy.

If that is how you feel, read on a bit further into Paul's letter:

> 'As God's fellow workers we urge you not to receive God's grace in vain. For he says, "In the time of my favour I heard you, and on the day of salvation I helped you." I tell you, now is the time of God's favour, now is the day of salvation.'
>
> *2 Corinthians 6:1–2*

God's help and salvation are available to us *now*. Paul

underlines this by quoting Isaiah 49:8 but changing the tenses. Isaiah says the Lord *will* hear and *will* help. Paul says God *has* heard and *has* helped. Therefore, Paul urges them not to receive God's grace and help in vain. *Now* is the day of opportunity and the chance to change.

But how can we find the motivation to change? When we are ready to give up hope, just then we find the help we need through God's grace. The 4,000 delegates from about 190 countries who attended the Lausanne II Congress in 1990, heard the testimony of Pastor Chang from China. He was arrested during the cultural revolution, but would not give up his faith. As a result he was forced to work in a cesspit. Alone amidst the stench and filth of human waste, he was content with a full and joyful heart to recite the psalms and praise the Lord Jesus *for nine years*. Each day proved to be a day of God's grace and salvation for that pastor.

In December 1978 Arthur Gaiger was assaulted and blinded on his own front door step, as a young motor cyclist threw hydrochloric acid in his face. There followed a painful time of many adjustments. Arthur had to come to the point of being able to forgive the young attacker and the instigator behind the attack. He knew times of self-pity and depression, but he learned to move out even in that darkness, putting his hand into the hand of God. In his situation, God's daily guidance was 'better than a light and safer than a known way.'

Pastor Chang and Arthur Gaiger – thousands of miles apart – had each learned to draw upon the grace of God to give them hope. Ronald, Peter and Lucy are also learning to do so. Mark and Julie still struggle.

The pressures of human weakness might lead us into despair, and to give up hope of achieving anything worthwhile for God. But we have seen in this chapter that the Christian is able to look at life through very different eyes. Everything that Jesus made possible for us he achieved only *through* his own human weakness and death, not in spite of it. With the eyes of faith we can see that the best is yet to be; as we focus our attention on Jesus we will feel the desire to please him spurring us on; a healthy fear of God will remind us that we are accountable to God for what we do with our days; and, even if then we still fail (and we will!), we have God's promise of grace, renewed to us daily, never rationed, and never withheld.

5

THE PRESSURE

OF

DIVIDED

LOYALTIES

In a family where Dad doesn't get on too well with the children, it's Mum who has to cope with the tensions. She wants to be loyal and loving to her husband; she also has the best interests of the children at heart. She's torn in two.

The Christian teacher or nurse has the welfare of her students or patients in mind. But her Trades Union calls her to come out on strike for the good of the whole profession.

The Christian minister or pastor, faces one section of the church asking for one course of action, while another group feels that a different course of action is better.

Many married couples have very full commitments to their local church. They could be out at different meetings every night of the week. But their own personal needs demand that they have some time at home together.

Young people finding their feet in life feel the pull

of their Christian friends on the one hand and their non-Christian friends on the other.

Life is full of conflicting demands.

As he continued to write to the church at Corinth, Paul gives us some practical points to help us deal with these daily conflicts of loyalty.

SORT OUT WHO IS BOSS!

When we were in our Sheffield parish it was the custom for the whole Church to walk in procession around the parish on Whit Monday. We would stop at two or three strategic points to sing a well-known hymn, and to preach for a few minutes. On one occasion, as we reached almost the end of the walk on a hot day, and with sore feet, I decided to speak about the challenge of Elijah to the people of Israel. They were undecided whether to worship and follow the local Baals (or gods) or whether to obey and follow the living God. Elijah's question was, 'Why are you limping between two opinions?'

Some of us were limping physically; maybe some of us, too, were limping spiritually from the pressure of divided loyalties.

Paul took pains to explain to the Corinthians how crucial it is to be clear about who is boss in our lives, and showed what it had meant in his own life:

> 'We put no stumbling-block in anyone's path, so that
> our ministry will not be discredited. Rather, as
> servants of God we commend ourselves in every way:
> in great endurance; in troubles, hardships and
> distresses; in beatings, imprisonments and riots; in

hard work, sleepless nights and hunger; in purity, understanding, patience and kindness; in the Holy Spirit and in sincere love; in truthful speech and in the power of God; with weapons of righteousness in the right hand and in the left; through glory and dishonour, bad report and good report; genuine, yet regarded as impostors; known, yet regarded as unknown; dying, and yet we live on; beaten, and yet not killed; sorrowful, yet always rejoicing; poor, yet making many rich; having nothing, and yet possessing everything.'   *2 Corinthians 6:3–10*

It is clear from other letters he wrote, that for Paul, Jesus was his Lord. He wrote to the Christians at Rome: 'Therefore, I urge you brothers, in view of God's mercy, to offer your bodies as living sacrifices . . . Do not conform any longer to the pattern of this world' (Romans 12:1–2). To the Church at Colossae he had written: 'So then, just as you received Christ Jesus as Lord, continue to live in him' (Colossians 2:6). He had explained to the Corinthians that they would not be effective Christians unless Jesus was clearly their Lord (1 Corinthians 12:3).

Jesus said that no one can serve two masters. 'Either he will hate the one and love the other, or he will be devoted to the one and despise the other. You cannot serve both God and Money' (Matthew 6:24). Paul could never have put up with the extreme hardships of his ministry had he been in the slightest doubt about whether he wanted Jesus to be Lord of his life. Having settled matters once and for all that Jesus was his master, he was willing and able to face the hard choices rather than go for the soft option – whether that meant facing calamities, imprisonment, beatings or hunger.

Clarify your priorities

Such single-mindedness made it a lot easier for Paul to sort out his priorities when faced with a choice. When conflicting demands were made on him, he knew that:

- Whatever decision he made, it should not discredit his ministry as a preacher of the gospel.
- He, and those who worked with him, were to act as faithful 'servants of God'.
- He would do all that he could to commend himself both to the Lord and the Corinthians in his actions and decisions.

He realised that when the pressure was on him, he was not to fall back on delay and compromise, but to use the spiritual weapons that God had given him. Paul would be patient and forbearing towards those who let him down. He would be kind when other people were unkind, hurtful or spiteful. He would act out of genuine love, when others acted out of self-interest.

The result of this is clear. If we have similar priorities to those of Paul, the world will probably criticise, and will certainly not understand. Paul's choice of priorities would have seemed just as odd to his contemporaries as they do to ours. In the world's eyes they are priorities which automatically relegate us to the position of nobodies having nothing and wasting our lives. Paul, after all, could have continued as a zealous Pharisee and teacher, and made a big name for himself had he not thrown it all in to follow Jesus. But which is more important – the assessment of other people or the assessment of God? For God saw Paul – and those who choose the same priorities as Paul – as most definitely a Somebody, rich through Jesus, and spending his life in the most purposeful way possible.

Sit loose to expectations

The fact that other people thought like this about him didn't worry Paul. He had settled in his own mind that pleasing Jesus was what mattered most: 'We make it our goal to please him.'

The leaders of our own Church live very busy lives. Each one knows the pressure of conflicting loyalties. They are all busy in their work – in the Civil Service, in business or in accountancy. There are many meetings they *could* attend in the life of the Church; and they all have family responsibilities and their own lives to lead.

In many Churches, the number of meetings you attend is taken as an indication of your loyalty to the Church and commitment to Christ. We make it known that this is not the case with us. If, for some reason, one of the Church leaders is not present at a meeting, however important it may be, he is not accused of letting the side down, because we have together agreed that *Jesus* – not the Church's agenda – is Lord, and each of us seeks to obey his leading. This may well mean that a person should spend an evening with his wife or family rather than at a Church meeting. It is for him to decide, before God, what Jesus is calling him to do.

Dr Moses Tay, Bishop of Singapore, asks this question each day: 'Lord, what is the Number One thing you want me to do today?' If we ask the same question and listen carefully to the reply, we may be surprised to discover that our Lord's agenda is not always the one that either we or others would expect.

Work for openness

When our loyalties are divided and we feel pulled in two different directions, it is very easy for misunder-standings and recriminations to arise. The Corinthians felt unsure of Paul because they couldn't make out quite what his priorities were. So they grew distrustful of him and began to be a bit cagey in their contact with him. This misunderstanding really hurt Paul and he had to write to them about it:

> 'We have spoken freely to you, Corinthians, and
> opened wide our hearts to you. We are not
> withholding our affection from you, but you are
> withholding yours from us. As a fair exchange – I
> speak as to my children – open wide your hearts
> also.'   *2 Corinthians 6:11–13*

Paul was aware that, in their uncertainty, the Corinthi-ans could be easily influenced by various people. Some criticised Paul very freely and were probably encourag-ing the Corinthian Church to be cold towards him. 'Don't listen to him!' they would have advised. But Paul urges them to be open and honest with him. He has opened his heart to them. Was it not now fair that they should open their hearts in love and response to him?

BE WISE IN YOUR PARTNERSHIPS

Paul was urging the Corinthians not only to open their hearts to him, but also to open their hearts and lives to the Lord and be utterly committed to Jesus. To this end he appeals to them to watch their relationships and not to create unnecessary pulls of loyalty for themselves:

'Do not be yoked together with unbelievers. For what do righteousness and wickedness have in common? Or what fellowship can light have with darkness? What harmony is there between Christ and Belial? What does a believer have in common with an unbeliever? What agreement is there between the temple of God and idols? For we are the temple of the living God. As God has said: "I will live with them and walk among them, and I will be their God, and they will be my people."

"Therefore come out from them and be separate, says the Lord.

Touch no unclean thing, and I will receive you."

"I will be a Father to you, and you will be my sons and daughters, says the Lord Almighty."

Since we have these promises, dear friends, let us purify ourselves from everything that contaminates body and spirit, perfecting holiness out of reverence for God.'   *2 Corinthians 6:14–7:1*

Choosing your partner

At the start of these verses, Paul is referring to Leviticus 19:19. There, God's people were instructed not to yoke different types of animals together. Two bulls of the same weight, height and size would pull the double yoke easily. However, if the farmer yoked together different animals of different natures, sizes and strengths, the plough would be pulled unevenly and in different directions. The yoke would chafe the necks of the animals concerned, and there would be pain and frustration all round.

There is pain and frustration when human beings are partnered together wrongly.

Each day of the week we are called to work with and alongside people who are not necessarily Christians: our colleagues and bosses at work, for example, or the voluntary services in our local community. We are asked for practical help and financial support from all manner of charities and pressure groups: Greenpeace, Oxfam, Save the Children, CAFOD, the World Wide Fund for Nature.

Some Christians have taken Paul's words here to mean that we should never associate, however loosely, with such organisations or voluntary services. And, they say, if we can't find a Christian firm to work for, we're better starting our own small business than 'yoking ourselves unequally' with a non-Christian company.

But this is not what Paul is saying. If we felt that we couldn't associate with a group – of whatever nature – unless we were completely in agreement with them, then, as Paul says in an earlier letter to the Corinthians, 'we would have to leave this world'! (1 Corinthians 5:10)

On the contrary, where we see that things aren't as ethical or above board as they should be, it is our task as 'the salt of the earth' and 'the light of the world' to get in there and bring a healthier and clearer understanding of our responsibilities to one another as human beings made in the image of God.

However, if we find ourselves in partnership with a group or a business whose methods are shady or wrong, then we should pull out from that group and break off our association. A young architect had established an unofficial partnership with another firm of architects. They shared the same staff and financial officers. The Christian was planning to enter into a legal partnership. Fortunately, it was discovered that his 'partnership firm' was keeping two sets of books and engaging in shady deals. The young Christian architect broke off all links with them, for the well-being of his professional work and career. It is this sort of partnership that Paul would describe as an 'unequal yoking'.

But there are many things on which Christians and non-Christians can agree, and many areas of life where we can work together for the good of society and to our mutual enrichment – and the New Testament encourages us to do this. Paul's point is, rather, that we should not think of entering into partnership with those whose views and goals are diametrically opposed to those of Christ.

In today's terms, then, there are perhaps three types of particularly close partnership where it is important for us to exercise great care: the marriage partnership, the business partnership and the 'ideological' partnership.

It is my privilege to conduct many weddings at church. Sadly, there have been times when a Christian man has married a girl who had no interest in Jesus. Often it is the other way round. The Christian girl has tried to persuade others, having first 'convinced herself', that it is all right for her to marry this non-Christian man. Very quickly her love for Jesus grows cold. Her church going declines, her Bible reading and prayer life is starved, and her spiritual life is almost snuffed out. She has been unequally yoked.

The same is true for Christians in business who decide that their partners need not be Christians, nor need share common ethical standards. But how does the Christian respond, then, when the accounts are not quite right? What does he say when unethical deals are planned and some dubious advertising material is printed? His loyalties are divided between following Christ and remaining loyal to his business partner.

While we understand the meaning of marriage and business partnerships, it is not always easy to perceive our 'ideological' partnerships. The term relates to the ideas and thinking of different groups. It can range from the pressures young people face at school, when they all want to be different but, strangely, all end up wearing exactly the same sort of clothes! There are the pressures exerted on the readers of the same newspapers — whether it be the *Daily Mirror* or the *Independent*. Trades Unions bring pressures to bear on their members. There are great pressures on those in business and the money markets: behind all the hectic activity, the large salaries and the fast lifestyles, is the pressure to make money and to increase the profits of the firms.

There are subtle religious ideological pressures. How does the Christian react to inter-faith services and activities? Should we support the work and aims of the World Wide Fund for Nature, which is concerned with ecology and yet seems to espouse some New Age ideas in its literature? There will be social pressures to conform to the standards of the area where we live, so far as the education of our children is concerned, what sort of car we drive, the size of our house and the sort of holidays we take.

This is the world in which we have to face pressure, and in which we are called upon to work out exactly what our partnerships should be and how far they should go. So Paul asks some searching questions: 'What do righteousness and wickedness have in common? What fellowship does light have with darkness? What harmony is there between Christ and Belial — the chief of demons? How can a believer and an unbeliever share the same Christian discipleship?' Paul is clearly putting the emphasis on the fact that there can be no basic agreement and harmony between two people whose fundamental loyalties are diametrically opposed.

Clearing muddied waters

If you are currently in a close partnership which you feel is hindering your discipleship and compromising your witness as a Christian, what can you do about it? Some partnerships can't be easily or quickly broken – nor should they be. You may not be able to get free from a legally binding business agreement for some time. And then it may be personally and financially costly to do so.

The Christian girl who has married an atheist husband can't suddenly go back on her promises and break her vows. However, she can repent before God for what she has done. She can begin to pray that the Lord will bring her husband to a faith in Christ. She can seek to honour and love Jesus. She can begin to love her husband with the love of Jesus.

There are some partnerships, however, that can and should be broken quickly. Where that is possible Paul issues five commands, some negative and some positive:

- 'Come out from them.' Break off the relationship. Don't go on seeing them on the same basis as you did previously.
- 'Be separate.' We are to be separate from anything that would damage our relationship with Jesus, or compromise our worship of him. If we have been set

apart as God's people, and he has pledged himself to be our God, how can we have any other gods?

● 'Touch no unclean thing.' It's 'hands off' anything that would corrupt us. You stop at a motorway service station to buy some food and drinks during a break in the journey. If you go into the shops do you allow your eyes to run over the papers and magazines on the top shelf? Do you know there are certain areas that you should not 'touch' with your eyes? The old nature within us wants to look. Our obedience to Jesus helps us to have nothing to do with anything that would corrupt us, taking the edge off our desire to please Jesus alone.

● 'Purify ourselves from everything that contaminates body and spirit.' Not only are we God's people, but God is our Father and we are his children. We don't want to do anything that would spoil our enjoyment of that fatherly relationship. For example, do we take care over the programmes we watch on TV? Many are very good. Others appear to be a waste of time and have no spiritual or personal benefit. Our aim, rather, is to . . .

● 'perfect holiness out of reverence for God.' Because we love and fear God (in the right sense that we have already noted), we shall want to become more like Jesus day by day. He was perfect holiness. So we may well find that the snappy reply to someone who has snapped at us, now gives way to a more gracious and loving reply. The tasks we couldn't be bothered to do because we were too proud, we now tackle with a willing spirit. The car that we would never lend to anyone else, because it was 'mine', we are now willing to lend in order to help someone out.

RENEW YOUR COMMITMENT

All the way through this first part of the letter – from chapters one to seven – Paul has been trying to resolve the tangled relationship he has with the Corinthian church. They have been critical of him, accusing him of being inconsistent and inferior to the 'super-apostles' around in Corinth at the time. Paul's own anxiety is to get on with the work of preaching the gospel, and to complete gathering in the collection that was started last year. At the same time, Paul has to rebuke one of the church members for sexual sin and for spoiling the fellowship between members.

They were all feeling under pressure! Paul has been wondering how the Corinthians responded to the harsh letter he had written to them earlier and which Titus had delivered. While he was waiting for Titus' response he was again restless in mind and spirit. But now that Titus has caught up with him and brought him a favourable report, Paul feels that now is the time to settle the tensions between himself and the church, and the divided loyalties that have affected the church members.

How is it to be done? Paul urges the move to come on their side. *He* is ready for reconciliation; are they? He urges the church to open their hearts to him, even though he seems to have acted harshly. He claims that he has wronged no one, corrupted no one, and taken advantage of no one. He is in the clear. There is nothing *he* has got to put right. Now it is up to the Corinthians. He challenges them to face up to the process of recovery:

> 'Even if I caused you sorrow by my letter, I do not regret it. Though I did regret it – I see that my letter hurt you, but only for a little while – yet now I am

happy, not because you were made sorry, but because your sorrow led you to repentance. For you became sorrowful as God intended and so were not harmed in any way by us. Godly sorrow brings repentance that leads to salvation and leaves no regret, but worldly sorrow brings death. See what this godly sorrow has produced in you: what earnestness, what eagerness to clear yourselves, what indignation, what alarm, what longing, what concern, what readiness to see justice done . . . By all this we are encouraged.

In addition to our own encouragement, we were especially delighted to see how happy Titus was, because his spirit has been refreshed by all of you.'

2 Corinthians 7:8–11, 13

The Corinthians needed to reaffirm their commitment to Christ as their Lord, and to Paul as their brother. This renewal of their commitment would come about through a process of 'recovery' from their divided state.

When you fall off a bicycle, there is a simple process of recovery. You pick yourself up, dust yourself down, pick up your bike, and get back on. It's much the same for anyone learning to ride a horse.

The process of recovery

If we become ill, there is a process of recovery that involves rest, medication and practical help. If we become spiritually 'ill', out of sorts with the Lord and our fellow Christians, there is also a process of recovery. It has five stages:

- *Rebellion.* That, like physical illness, is the original

problem. And like illness, it needs to be recognised before it can be treated.

● *Rebuke*. Paul had to show that what had been done in the Corinthian church was wrong. Lovingly, he had to confront sin, like a doctor gently informing his patient of the nature of his illness. Being in a state of sin puts us under pressure, and the failure to recognise and confront it puts us under more pressure. We compromise with sin, like a person who refuses to admit she is ill and then tries to adapt the rest of her life around her new limitations, insisting that everything is 'normal'. If we pretend that the sin does not exist, we are living with divided loyalties, professing one standard yet actually following another.

● *Repentance*. Paul makes a distinction between 'worldly regret' and 'godly sorrow.' Regret is being sorry that we got into trouble. It's being fed up that we have been found out, rather than being sorry that we did what we did. Godly sorrow, on the other hand, is genuine sorrow and repentance that we have not only hurt ourselves and others, but also God himself. We begin to see ourselves as God sees us. Worldly regret is mere self-pity and self-disgust.

Paul is excited that the repentance of the Corinthian fellowship has been so genuine. They are really eager to clear their own name, as well as ready to see justice done.

● *Restoration*. Local churches are not good at this. We are much better at remembering other people's faults than knowing how to restore one another in a spirit of gentleness.

We remember very clearly that couple who were involved in adultery, that young woman who had an abortion, that young man who played around with the prostitutes, that couple who got themselves into trouble with the police, that man who can't be trusted, that son who drank too much! That shows restoration has not taken place! We have no business to recall past failures. God doesn't do that with us; we are told that he remembers our sin no more. We need to pray for a good memory of God's grace to us, and a divine 'forgettery' to cover the sins of other people. When that happens there will be the final stage in this process of recovery:

● *Rejoicing*. There is real joy in knowing that sins have been forgiven. The sinner is glad, the whole church is glad, the mediators are glad.

How can we apply this cycle of restoration in our own relationships? Here are some examples you may find familiar! Think about your response to these situations, taking the cycle of restoration into account:

● Mum and Dad have waited up till the early hours for their teenage son. His sister has been worrying, too, and getting the brunt of her parents' anxiety. The teenager is eventually brought home by a friend at 3 am, hopelessly drunk. How would you like to see each respond to that situation?

● A member of the family has been out on a credit card spending spree. Now it has all come to light and the rest of the family feel mortified and badly let down. How should they respond?

● A member of the church has not been attending for some time because he has been having an affair. But now he has ended it and wants to re-enter fellowship with the church. The church members aren't sure what to do. How would you advise them?

● A woman is under severe pressure and has drifted away from church, saying that Christianity offers nothing for people like her. If you were a member of that church, what would you do?

• One of your colleagues at work has been giving you a hard time and has almost caused you to lose your job. How will this 'cycle of recovery' help you plan how to act in relation to that person?

So Paul can end this part of the letter on a note of joy and encouragement. Stress and pressure from divided loyalties are part of human experience, but there is a way through.

First, we need to be clear in our commitment to Jesus as Lord of every aspect of our lives. Whatever the cost, *his* way is to be *our* way.

Second, we need to watch our relationships, strengthening those that support us in our commitment to Christ and staying clear of those that pull us away from him.

Third, we need to know what to do when things go wrong in our lives. There is a way back to recovery from rebellion, rebuke and repentance, to restoration and rejoicing. When we live like this we shall no longer destroy one another, but will be able to encourage and build one another up in love.

6

THE PRESSURE

OF

MONEY

Money and sex are the two things that cause probably
most of the trouble in life. We have already seen that
Paul had to deal with some sexual problems in the
church at Corinth. Those were happily resolved. Now
he talks about money.

Money is never out of the news. A very few people
– those who have won huge prizes on the pools, or
who command very high salaries – may suffer from
the pressure of too much money! Others make it their
business to raise money, perhaps through Comic Relief
or the BBC's 'Children in Need' appeal. Thousands
work and give to children and adults in great need in
this country and other parts of the world.

But most of us are constantly seeking to make ends
meet with ever rising costs, national and local taxes and
VAT increases. That tatty carpet will have to last
another year; the next holiday will have to be at Grand-
ma's rather than in Spain; and our friends will have to
make do with last year's Christmas cards recycled for
this year! And when it comes to Christian giving we are
constantly reminded of the needs of our own church
locally, the diocese (if we are a member of the Church

of England) and of missionary and aid societies. They, too, wonder each year whether they will be able to make ends meet.

It's fascinating to discover from Paul's letter that, first, money pressures are not new, and secondly, that Paul has a surprising way of dealing with them.

GIVE IT AWAY!

In Acts 11:27–30, we see the first example of Christian Aid or Tear Fund in action. News had come to the church at Antioch in Asia Minor that the Christians at the mother church in Jerusalem were hard pressed financially. It wasn't their fault. These Jewish Christians had been hit hard by the outbreak of famine during the reign of Emperor Claudius (AD 41–54). The Gentile Christians in Antioch planned to have a collection and send it to Jerusalem. So Gentile money was going to help Jewish Christians. Paul continues to canvass aid from the Corinthian church. Then the churches in Macedonia also begged to have a part in the collection.

What was astonishing about that was that the churches in Macedonia were not rich and well off, in fact, exactly the opposite. They faced severe, extreme poverty, but they were able to give because they had already given themselves in totality to the Lord. Paul tells the Corinthians about them, and urges them to carry on making the collection they had started the previous year:

> 'And now, brothers, we want you to know about the grace that God has given the Macedonian churches. Out of the most severe trial, their overflowing joy

and their extreme poverty welled up in rich
generosity. For I testify that they gave as much as
they were able, and even beyond their ability.
Entirely on their own, they urgently pleaded with us
for the privilege of sharing in this service to the
saints. And they did not do as we expected, but they
gave themselves first to the Lord and then to us in
keeping with God's will. So we urged Titus, since he
had earlier made a beginning, to bring also to
completion this act of grace on your part. But just as
you excel in everything – in faith, in speech, in
knowledge, in complete earnestness and in your love
for us – see that you also excel in this grace of
giving.'   *2 Corinthians 8:1–7*

What an example! But it is one that could be paralleled
many times over in Christian homes and churches
today.

I have been humbled to hear stories of Christians
in Latin America entertaining visitors and giving literally all the food that remained in the house to their
guests, not knowing how they were going to feed themselves for the rest of the week.

Near us in East London is a house called Mill
Grove, where you can find an outstanding example of
Christian love and care. Formerly known as White's
Homes, it is a house set up for the care of young people,
and its staff have done so for many years. They are
supported entirely by voluntary giving. Each year Mill
Grove holds a Thanksgiving Service in our church. One
year I was privileged to speak at that service and to
read the letters that came in from ordinary Christians
around the country who had given to it. The letters
contained such comments as: 'Humanly speaking, it is

more than I can afford', 'He has been faithful', 'My God is your God, and our God is able', 'There is enough left over to cover my burial and I am happy.'

Two missionaries out with CMS in Africa and working at a theological college, had to come to terms with the different standards of living between the West and the rest of the world, between North and South. They wrote home, 'We certainly didn't think of ourselves as rich before we came here. But we saw that what we took for granted in Europe is beyond the means of all but the richest here.'

Why should I give?

The example of the Christians in Macedonia, the supporters of Mill Grove and those in situations of poverty overseas, raises the question, 'Why should I give?' Paul gives us three answers.

Look at what the collection can achieve!
Paul uses some remarkable words to describe the collection made by the Macedonians. We might have referred to it as taking an offering, passing round the hat, or having a whip round! But the Macedonians saw it very differently. They talked about it in terms of:

• Exercising a gift. The Greek word for gift is *charis*, and they saw the ability to give as being a charismatic gift. As the ability and desire to give had been given to them by God – they were determined to exercise that gift to bring God's grace to others!
• A practical expression of fellowship. All our talk of fellowship with other Christians is fairly hollow unless we are prepared to put our money where our mouth is.

The Macedonians seized the chance to make their verbal fellowship a tangible fellowship.

● Serving others. In pledging themselves to the service of Christ, the Macedonians also pledged themselves to the service of Christ's brothers and sisters. So when the opportunity arose to minister to their needs, they took it!

If we put the three key words together – grace or gift, fellowship and service – we get a definition of the collection as 'a demonstration of God's grace in the fellowship of the church to help serve and meet the needs of one another.' I wonder if that is how we usually see giving?

Look at Jesus!

> 'I am not commanding you, but I want to test the sincerity of your love by comparing it with the earnestness of others. For you know the grace of our Lord Jesus Christ, that though he was rich, yet for your sakes he became poor, so that you through his poverty might become rich.'
>
> *2 Corinthians 8:8–9*

The theme of 'God's grace' begins and ends this letter, and it comes seven times here in the space of nineteen verses! Grace is God's love and goodness to those in need – not because they deserve it, but simply because they need it. To see giving as an act of grace lifts it into the realm of what is lovely, good, beautiful and glorious.

But God's grace is shown supremely in the life of the Lord Jesus Christ.

Paul tells us about the *position* of Jesus: though he

was rich in glory and heaven, yet he was willing to become poor for our sakes. The *poverty* of Jesus was seen in his human birth, humble home and simple lifestyle. He swopped the creator's throne for the carpenter's bench, and a Roman cross. All this had a *purpose*: that through his poverty we might become rich. Paul teaches that there is an important *principle* here for all Christians to learn: we are to follow Christ in becoming poor so that others might become rich.

Look at yourself!

There was a third reason for the Macedonians giving as they did. They had taken a good, hard look at themselves and realised that all that they were – and all that they had – already belonged to the Lord.

Because of this they understood that giving involved more than their money, and so they consciously and deliberately first 'gave themselves to the Lord.' Once they had done that it was a comparatively small step to give him their things, too. For some people today, this will involve giving their time, their love and their home in hospitality. Others will give books so that Christians in other parts of the world will at least have a few.

Can I afford to give?

'Remember this: Whoever sows sparingly will also reap sparingly, and whoever sows generously will also reap generously. Each man should give what he has decided in his heart to give, not reluctantly or under compulsion, for God loves a cheerful giver. And God is able to make all grace abound to you,

so that in all things at all times, having all that you
need, you will abound in every good work. As it is
written:

> "He has scattered abroad his gifts to the poor;
> his righteousness endures for ever."

Now he who supplies seed to the sower and bread
for food will also supply and increase your store of
seed and will enlarge the harvest of your
righteousness. You will be made rich in every way
so that you can be generous on every occasion, and
through us your generosity will result in
thanksgiving to God.

This service that you perform is not only
supplying the needs of God's people but is also
overflowing in many expressions of thanks to God.
Because of the service by which you have proved
yourselves, men will praise God for the obedience
that accompanies your confession of the gospel of
Christ, and for your generosity in sharing with them
and with everyone else. And in their prayers for you
their hearts will go out to you, because of the
surpassing grace God has given you. Thanks be to
God for his indescribable gift!'

2 Corinthians 9:6–15

Isn't it more a matter of can we afford *not* to give?!
Paul spells out that real blessings are received by us as
well as the recipients – when we give in the right way.
The amazing truth is that when we face money pressures, the secret is to *give* rather than get! Getting is the
way of the world. Giving is the way of the Lord.

Paul tells the Corinthians that five blessings will
flow from their giving:

- They will meet the needs of others.
- They will cause people to be thankful to God.
- People will praise God for the way the lives of the Corinthians match up with the gospel they profess.
- The reality of their fellowship with their fellow Christians will be proved and deepened.
- Those who receive the gift will want to respond by praying for the Corinthians.

At our last Church Annual Meeting, we launched a scheme to rebuild our verger's house. It was cheaper to knock down and rebuild, than to completely refurbish it. I asked the Deputy Warden, Hugh, to give a word of encouragement to the congregation. He spoke first of all of the healing of his vocal chords that he had experienced as a result of prayer.

Then he went on to say: 'Some of us know about giving; some know a lot about giving. Others have never really tried it. I have to tell you that it's a very low-risk exercise. God loves a cheerful giver and God is able to provide you with every blessing in abundance, so he's going to look after you! You have nothing to worry about if you want to give; and if you want to give in a very big way, God will still look after you! I can't find any more encouraging words than that!' He had been quoting from these chapters in the letter as he spoke. It was a powerful testimony.

There are an increasing number of churches that are learning to give. One such church is not very far from us in the inner area of East London. The Vicar wrote that almost all the money the church needed comes to the church Treasurer through direct giving, mainly in the Sunday offerings. Their membership is about 130. When he began to teach about Christian giving, things began to change. Giving to missions was £216 in the first year. Ten years later it was nearer to £4,000. The church can now give away about the same amount as they need to meet their costs. Then he went on to speak about the blessing to the church:

'It would be difficult to separate the blessings of the individual from the blessings of the church over these years, for the blessings of the one are closely interrelated with the blessings of the other. When faced with the demands of biblical Christian giving, individuals have set out by asking, "Can God?" and finished by proving and saying, "God can." Those who started to tithe their income found that God repaid in a host of ways, and little faith became greater faith.

Straight biblical teaching was rewarded by more people being added to the Church and, as the congregation increased, so did the giving. We found that we were able to attempt projects on the church plant that could not have been thought possible before. It became a joy to allocate missionary money and to know that others enjoyed the benefit of our giving. It is a cause for great rejoicing that the giving of the home church helps in the conversion of people to Christ in foreign fields.

Overall we have learnt that when we are generous to God, he is no man's debtor and that in turn we always have more than enough to go on being generous. What St Paul said so long ago is true today: "God is able to provide you with every blessing in abundance, so that you may always have enough of everything and may provide in abundance for every good work" (2 Corinthians 9:8, RSV)'

Obviously, we need to plan our giving, and manage our money wisely. I receive many letters from a variety of Christian and charitable organisations asking for gifts. It's all too easy to harden one's heart; to tear up the appeal letter and consign it to the waste paper basket.

There are four things we could do with appeal letters like that:

- do nothing about it;
- pass it on to the church for action;
- write them a letter of encouragement;
- send off some money.

Each of these four responses has to be prayerfully considered and any one might be right. It is quite clear that we can't give to everything that comes our way. It is equally clear that we should respond to some needs that do come our way.

How much should I give?

Paul doesn't write about the pounds we should give. Rather, he writes about the principles we should follow when giving:

> 'And here is my advice about what is best for you in this matter: Last year you were the first not only to give but also to have the desire to do so. Now finish the work, so that your eager willingness to do it may be matched by your completion of it, according to your means. For if the willingness is there, the gift is acceptable according to what one has, not according to what he does not have.
>
> Our desire is not that others might be relieved while you are hard pressed, but that there might be equality. At the present time your plenty will supply

what they need, so that in turn their plenty will supply what you need. Then there will be equality, as it is written: "He that gathered much did not have too much, and he that gathered little did not have too little." '   *2 Corinthians 8:10–15*

● *Giving should be gladly done.* The Lord loves a cheerful giver. God takes more notice of the love in our hearts than the large amount in the bank. We are not to give reluctantly or under compulsion. Giving flows out of dedication to the Lord, rather than a sense of duty to the work.

● *The purpose of giving is to achieve equality and inter-dependence.* Burdens need to be shared. Paul teaches equality on the grounds of fairness. He also taught it from the experience of the Children of Israel gathering the manna in the wilderness (Exodus 16:12). It seemed to be God's intention that those who gathered a lot should have nothing left over at the end of the day, while those who collected just a little found it was enough.

So Paul expected that the rich would give to the poor, and that the relatively poor would give to the absolutely poor.

But he is also aware that circumstances can change very quickly. Those who are rich today could become poor tomorrow – it had happened to the Christians at Jerusalem. In turn, the poor might become rich. They would then be able to return God's grace to those who had originally given to them. The principle is that we are to share what we have with those in need.

● *What we sow, we shall reap.* When we give, God will give back to us. The more we give, the more we get. That is the clear message: 'God is able to make all grace abound to us, so that in all things at all times, having all that you need, you will abound in every good deed.'

What about the 'Prosperity Gospel'?

Some Christians have got themselves into trouble, financially and spiritually, because they have believed the 'Prosperity Gospel'. Put simply, this teaches that God wants us to be financially wealthy and materially comfortable. After all, we are his children, and what father would give his children any less than the best he could afford? So those who teach this way of thinking teach that all Christians, if they are 'right with the Lord', will be prosperous. What's more, the more they give, the more the Lord will bless them financially. And that would seem to arise from these verses.

Proponents of this view are right in that there is not necessarily anything wrong with being rich and prosperous. There are examples of people in the Bible whom God chose to bless materially – Abraham and Job, for instance.

But consider the following:

• Our attitude to riches, and how we use them, is more important than how much we possess. Remember Paul's earlier point about divided loyalties and the need to make sure that Jesus is 'boss' in our lives? Our goal should be to please him, not to get rich. Paul had learnt to be content, whether he had much or little (Philippians 4:11–13).

• The 'get as you give' theory of the Prosperity Gospel does not seem to be borne out in practice. Many Third-world Christians are in great need, though they give generously.

● Jesus calls us to a costly discipleship. If we are following him closely we are more likely to find ourselves carrying a cross than a cushion!

Where Prosperity teaching goes wrong in its interpretation of this passage is that it misses the thrust of Paul's teaching. Paul is talking of *recycling* money, not accumulating it. As we give, so we will receive. As we receive so we will be able to go on giving. As we go on giving, so we will continue to receive, and therefore go on giving. The Christian's money should be recycled money!

MANAGE IT PROPERLY

Pressure over money isn't concerned only with what we give. It also involves how we manage it.

> 'I thank God, who put into the heart of Titus the same concern I have for you. For Titus not only welcomed our appeal, but he is coming to you with much enthusiasm and on his own initiative. And we are sending along with him the brother who is praised by all the churches for his service to the gospel. What is more, he was chosen by the churches to accompany us as we carry the offering, which we administer in order to honour the Lord himself and to show our eagerness to help. We want to avoid any criticism of the way we administer this liberal gift. For we are taking pains to do what is right, not only in the eyes of the Lord but also in the eyes of men.

> In addition, we are sending with them our brother who has often proved to us in many ways that he is zealous, and now even more so because of his great confidence in you. As for Titus, he is my partner and fellow-worker among you; as for our brothers, they are representatives of the churches and an honour to Christ. Therefore show these men the proof of your love and the reason for our pride in you, so that the churches can see it.'
>
> *2 Corinthians 8:16–24*

Paul is very practical and down to earth. There are three final comments that he makes about handling money so that we are not under pressure from it.

Look after your financial affairs

Money is not something 'dirty' or corrupting. If we have money, we should steward it wisely – making sure we are providing properly for our families, and are able to give to others. Paul mentions three men who were going to take the collection to the Christians at Jerusalem. We don't know them by name, but we do know that they were trustworthy, reliable, and competent to look after money.

Sadly, that isn't true about everyone who handles money. We are under increasing pressure from advertisements, mailshots, loan sharks, insurance policies and investments to put our money into other people's hands for the best returns. It doesn't always work out like that. Perhaps it is our Christian responsibility to find a trustworthy accountant who will help us manage our money wisely.

Keep the account books straight

Paul is not only concerned to affirm the men who are managing the money. He was concerned that the money was distributed in the best way. Some Christians get into financial troubles because they don't take proper care over how they spend it. They are slipshod and careless at keeping records. If they have it in their pocket or bank, they spend it. If they need something, or something suddenly catches their eyes, they'll buy it with their credit card. That is not good administration of money.

Three times a year we have a marriage preparation weekend for couples getting married at church. Part of one session is devoted to budgeting the couple's finances. We set out a sample budget – everything is included – so that a couple can see how to log in their income and outgoings, and will get some idea of what they are likely to spend in a month or a year. In that way many pressures will be avoided. The good habits of handling money begin.

Failure to keep household accounts leads many into debt. It can take only weeks to fall into debt, but years to climb out of it.

Not everyone feels budgeting to be easy. This may be due to temperament or the irregular receipt of their income. Such budgeting for some Christians can become a strait jacket and a burden rather than a help. Whatever alternative methods other Christians may use, it is important that they don't spend what they haven't got and that they are willing and able to take advice, from time to time, about their financial arrangements and their provision both for the present and for the future.

Invite in the heavenly auditor

Before I was ordained, I was training to be an auditor in the Civil Service. I would check over the rent and rate accounts of local authorities in Hampshire to ensure that the money received was right, and properly accounted for. John Stott has suggested that we need to allow God to do the same thing with our own money:

> 'We have got to keep accounts, so that we can examine them at least once a year prayerfully. Let the Holy Spirit be our auditor. Then we shall be able to consider if our expenditure is wise, moderate, balanced and pleasing to God.'

It's good to check up each year on how we are using the money God has given us. It will help to ensure that our giving is honouring to the Lord.

Most of us would like to have more money. But it is not always more money that we need. Better managing and wiser use of what we have, may be part of the answer. Paul urges good accounting, wise budgeting, and joyful giving as he shares this outstanding example of the churches of Macedonia and Corinth.

Yet behind it all was the example of the Lord Jesus. He closes this section of his letter with the exclamation, 'Thanks be to God for his indescribable gift!' Paul uses a word found only here, and nowhere else in the New Testament or in classical Greek, to describe the Lord Jesus. That surely is right. Jesus is an indescribably valuable and unique gift to us.

It is the example of his self-giving that will guide and inspire us in our giving and our handling of money, so that we become freer from its mastery and pressure in our lives.

7

THE PRESSURE
OF
CRITICISM

'I don't like the colour of your shirt.' 'I don't like the way you just spoke to me.' 'I don't think you are telling me the truth.' 'You can't trust the Government.' 'They don't mean what they say.' 'Why don't the Bishops speak out more on national issues?' 'Why did we have that hymn tune that nobody knew?' 'Why can't we have the old service?' 'Why doesn't she make her children behave properly?'

Criticism. None of us escapes it. Probably most of us are free in giving it.

Criticism puts each of us under pressure. *Was* I wrong? *Should* I have done something different? *Was* I unkind? Sometimes we answer criticism with more criticism, and the situation gets worse. Sometimes a still tongue is the wisest tongue.

Criticism is concerned with what people say and think. It is other people's reaction to our action. Paul was not free from it, and it is helpful to discover how he handled its pressure.

UNDER ATTACK

Paul faced three attacks: from his fellow Christians at Corinth, from Satan, and from a group who had become known as the 'super-apostles'.

Criticised by other Christians

'By the meekness and gentleness of Christ, I appeal to you – I, Paul, who am "timid" when face to face with you, but "bold" when away! I beg you that when I come I may not have to be as bold as I expect to be towards some people who think that we live by the standards of this world . . . we will be ready to punish every act of disobedience, once your obedience is complete.'

2 Corinthians 10:1–2, 6

'Was it a sin for me to lower myself in order to elevate you by preaching the gospel of God to you free of charge? I robbed other churches by receiving support from them so as to serve you. And when I was with you and needed something, I was not a burden to anyone, for the brothers who came from Macedonia supplied what I needed. I have kept myself from being a burden to you in any way, and will continue to do so. As surely as the truth of Christ is in me, nobody in the regions of Achaia will stop this boasting of mine. Why? Because I do not love you? God knows I do!'

2 Corinthians 11:7–11

Paul faced various accusations:

'You're inconsistent!'

Paul was accused of being inconsistent and lacking in moral courage. He was a moral coward, they said, strict enough in his letters, but when with them in person he seemed to climb down from his threats. He said one thing when he was present, but another when he was away. He was accused of being one person in public, another in private.

This is a criticism that bites deep. We all know there is an element of truth in it when it is directed at us, because we don't always live up to our own standards or practice what we preach. The book, *Battered into Submission*, by James and Phyllis Alsdurf (Crowborough: Highland Books, 1990), is a disturbing book about the behaviour of Christian leaders and husbands towards their wives. Although written in America, it reflects something of the scene in this country. While publicly preaching a gospel of peace, forgiveness and self-giving love, some Christian leaders are violent and abusive at home, criticising their wives for such things as the length of their skirts, the timing of a meal or the way they bring up the children.

Are we in danger of a similar inconsistency? In public we are charming; in private we are grumpy and morose. In public our words are kind, but behind our front doors we pull other Christians to pieces. We like to appear generous and open-hearted, when in reality we are mean in our thoughts and spirit.

'You're worldly!'

Second, Paul was accused by the Corinthians of living by the standards of the world rather than by Christian (their!) standards.

It's sometimes very difficult to know which of our

standards are biblical, and which are merely cultural. Older people who put on their Sunday best for church may well feel critical of younger people who turn up for morning worship in tee-shirt and jeans. Are the young people being worldly? Or are the older people confusing what their culture looks on as 'being properly dressed' with a right attitude of reverence?

Cardinal Hume has described this sort of judgmental criticism as one of the things most destructive of the unity of the church. Guitar music is 'worldly'. Organ playing is 'religious'! Even among Christians we can accuse one another of living by the standards of the world. In our thoughts – even if not by our words – we may criticise other Christians for the amount of money they spend on a holiday, or the way they use their time.

While we uphold the principle of freedom of speech, that doesn't mean we have liberty to say whatever we like about other people. Paul tells us that we are to stop using negative and destructive speech, and to say only those things that would encourage and help a fellow Christian (see Ephesians 4:25, 31 and Colossians 4:6). That should be even more true in our talking with non-Christians.

'You don't love us!'

Paul also had to face the accusation that he didn't love the Corinthian church because he wasn't willing to accept their financial help. The truth of the matter was that Paul didn't want to be a burden to them! He was prepared to work to pay his way while he stayed with them. The Corinthians, however, regarded this as a degrading thing for an apostle to do, and perhaps felt he was 'showing them up'. Whatever their reasons, they took it the wrong way. There are times when you just can't win! When that happens I find it best to commit the whole situation to the Lord. Allow him to be the judge of what is right or wrong and ask for his patience to control your heart and mind.

Criticised by Satan

> 'For though we live in the world, we do not wage war as the world does. The weapons we fight with are not the weapons of the world. On the contrary, they have divine power to demolish strongholds. We demolish arguments and every pretension that sets itself up against the knowledge of God, and we take captive every thought to make it obedient to Christ.'
> *2 Corinthians 10:4–5*

There is more about the work and attacks of Satan in this letter than in most other parts of the New Testament. Paul believed that Satan was real and out to do business. Jesus believed the same. They understood that he is a powerful foe, but they didn't think of him as equal with God. God is all-knowing, all-powerful, and present everywhere. The devil isn't like that. So it is not a matter of good and evil being equally pitted against each other. Nevertheless, Satan is a tiresome and active enemy.

One of his chief tactics is to attack a person's mind.

Our thoughts will come from one of three directions: from ourselves – ordinary, human thoughts; from God – special, lovely, pure and particularly incisive thoughts; or we may suddenly find that our thoughts are murderous, angry, dirty, horrible, impure and vicious. We are appalled at what we find rushing through our minds. Those thoughts may have been planted by Satan and certainly need to be brought captive to obey the teaching of Jesus. If they are not thoughts that we could think and speak out in the presence of Jesus, then we have to reject and dismiss them.

In this letter to the Corinthians, Paul shows there are a number of ways in which Satan attacks the mind:

- He dulls the minds of those who don't believe in Jesus, trying to stop them understanding what the gospel is all about and preventing them from realising how important it is (see 2 Corinthians 4:4–6).
- He disturbs the mind by placing unwholesome and destructive thoughts there (see 10:5).
- He tries to deceive young Christians and to pull them away from their new-found obedience to and love of Jesus. Paul describes this as being as underhand as trying to turn a young woman against the man to whom she has just been betrothed. In Jewish custom, a betrothal was far more binding than an engagement is to us today, so breaking the relationship at that point would be tantamount to divorce, and very destructive for the woman.

Satan seeks to drag new believers away from their commitment to Jesus. He undermines the certainty of their faith, tells them that they're not good enough to be Christians, tries to convince them they'll never be able to put up with the laughter of their friends. 'You won't be able to remain faithful to Jesus,' he says; 'it'll be too hard.'

- Satan is so subtle that he even disguises himself as an angel of light (see 11:14). He can make what is bad, look good to us. Shirley Maclaine, together with her brother, Warren Beatty, were once both Christians. Shirley, a brilliant American actress, singer and dancer, is now a world-known leader and teacher of New Age philosophy. Somewhere along the line Satan presented her with some teachings that looked especially pure and good. He deceived her as a young believer, and persuaded her that what was harmful was in fact harmless and very spiritual.

• Satan also tries to discourage the Christian who is making an impact for good in the world – in society, at work or in her family. He nags and harasses and throws up as much trouble as he can to wear that person down. Paul writes about it being like having a 'thorn in the flesh' (see 12:7–9).

It is abundantly clear that Satan attacks the minds of people. They may not yet be believers. They may be young Christians or mature Christians. The attacks will come in different forms, but the fact of the attacks is not to be denied.

Criticised by rivals

Attack number three came from another group in the city of Corinth. This was a group of men who lived there but didn't belong to the Church. They seem to have been the most persistent and troublesome group that Paul faced. They put themselves forward as apostles of Christ, they were eloquent speakers, and they did their best to undermine the authority of Paul:

> 'But I am afraid that just as Eve was deceived by the serpent's cunning, your minds may somehow be led astray from your sincere and pure devotion to Christ. For if someone comes to you and preaches a Jesus

other than the Jesus we preached, or if you receive a
different spirit from the one you received, or a
different gospel from the one you accepted, you put
up with it easily enough. But I do not think I am in
the least inferior to those "super-apostles". I may not
be a trained speaker, but I do have knowledge. We
have made this perfectly clear to you in every
way . . .

And I will keep on doing what I am doing in
order to cut the ground from under those who want
an opportunity to be considered equal with us in the
things they boast about.

For such men are false apostles, deceitful
workmen, masquerading as apostles of Christ. And
no wonder, for Satan himself masquerades as an
angel of light. It is not surprising, then, if his
servants masquerade as servants of righteousness.
Their end will be what their actions deserve.'

2 Corinthians 11:3–6, 12–15

Their strategy was to turn people's focus away from
the truth or otherwise of what they were saying, and to
focus it instead on comparing them with other Christian
leaders. And, by comparison, they were obviously an
impressive bunch. Their speech and presence were auth-
oritative. They ran their 'apostleship' on good business
terms, levying a fee for the message they gave, on the
grounds that if people had to pay for what they received
they would value it more highly. They had impeccable
Jewish ancestries, claimed impressive spiritual experiences and the ability to perform apostolic signs and
wonders (see 11:21–22; 12:1–6, 12). By all these means
they tried to discredit Paul, making him look small and
ineffective by comparison.

The temptation to make ourselves look taller by climbing on top of other people is still with us. We compare ourselves with others and conclude we are better than them, so assume we're doing OK! But we might still be falling very short of *God's* standards. Remember the parable of the Pharisee and the publican!

If one danger is to compare ourselves favourably with others, the opposite danger is to compare ourselves unfavourably with them. We think to ourselves: 'Why don't I feel as keen as they do about going to Spring Harvest? Why do they seem to be doing a better job bringing up their children? How come they get their prayers answered but so little happens when *I* pray? Why are exciting things always happening at their church but not at ours?'

Such unhelpful, but common enough, ways of comparing ourselves unfavourably with others in the Christian life can be both destructive and discouraging. Paul refuses to play that game. He will not compare himself with those 'super-apostles' – nor with anyone else. He won't commend himself in the same way as the super-apostles do either, nor measure himself by the same standards. Instead, Paul has something better to boast about, and a totally different yardstick against which to measure his performance:

> 'We do not dare to classify or compare ourselves with some who commend themselves. When they measure themselves by themselves and compare themselves with themselves, they are not wise. We, however, will not boast beyond proper limits, but will confine our boasting to the field God has assigned for us, a field that reaches even to you. We are not going too far in our boasting, as would be the case if we had not come to you, for we did get

as far as you with the gospel of Christ. Neither do we go beyond our limits by boasting of work done by others. Our hope is that, as your faith continues to grow, our area of activity among you will greatly expand, so that we can preach the gospel in the regions beyond you. For we do not want to boast about work already done in another man's territory. But, "Let him who boasts boast in the Lord." For it is not the one who commends himself who is approved, but the one whom the Lord commends.'
2 Corinthians 10:12–18

While others boasted in what they did, where they came from, who they were and what they had achieved, Paul boasted in who *Christ* is and what *he* has done. Sometimes people boast about what they have done in their Christian lives almost as if they are searching for assurance and security. They are trusting in what they have done or are doing. Paul used to do this; now he realises that his security and assurance are found in Christ, so he will boast only of Christ.

Paul knew that God had really and truly accepted him, because of what Christ had done. No longer did he look for acceptance – either with God or with other people – on the grounds of what he had done.

RESPONDING TO CRITICISM

Paul was attacked by the Corinthians (the flesh), by Satan (the devil) and by the super-apostles (the world). In each case he referred the criticism back to Christ; it was only his opinion that really mattered to Paul. Three important strategies for dealing with criticism emerge as Paul writes on.

Find your security in Jesus

> 'You are looking only on the surface of things. If anyone is confident that he belongs to Christ, he should consider again that we belong to Christ just as much as he.'   *2 Corinthians 10:8*

The thing that mattered to Paul, more than anything else, was that he belonged to Jesus. All he did stemmed from the security of that relationship. What matters most to you? If you were forced at gun-point to hand over your possessions, which would you keep till the very last moment because it is the thing you value most? The relationship that is most important in your life is probably one with the person who accepts you, affirms you, and gives you greatest security in your life. Jesus was more important to Paul than anything or anyone else in the whole world. Do you find that to be true for yourself? Is your personal security found in Jesus?

There are some basic needs that we all have. The need to belong, the need for security, the need to discover our purpose and identity in life. The answer to all these questions for Paul was to be found in Jesus. It was because he was secure in his relationship to Jesus that he was able to withstand the pressure of criticism and attack.

Use your spiritual weapons

Paul had been accused of living in a worldly fashion.

He was wrestling with the subtle attacks of the devil, but he was equipped with spiritual weapons that were capable of withstanding such criticism. He could win the battle.

Let's take a look at the main weapons we have for using against the devil's attack. They are mentioned in different parts of the New Testament:

• *Prayer.* I had the privilege recently of visiting a church in Wales where God is very much at work. People are getting converted and the church is growing. Church life generally in Wales is beginning to show fruit. Then I discovered that people in that particular church were meeting to pray at 6 am three times a week! They were also setting aside a day a month for prayer and fasting.

It is not always easy to explain why prayer works. The evidence is that when we work, *we* work; but when we pray *God* works.

• *Praise* is the second weapon. Praise helps us to see Jesus in proper perspective – as King of kings, Lord of lords, mighty and victorious. We realise again how great he is, and our faith is increased. Jesus is glorified. Satan can't stand us praising the Lord and he has to flee.

• *Love* is a remarkable weapon. We saw something of its results earlier in the story about Caesar Molebasti. From Africa comes also the story of Bishop Festo Kivengere's meeting with President Idi Amin. Amin's reign of terror in Uganda had led to many brutal murders and deaths. Festo was asked what he would do if he met Idi Amin, who presented him with a gun. Festo would reply, 'I think this is your weapon. Ours is love.'

• *Truth* – the word of God. Satan uses lies and deceit. The weapon against lies is truth. The Holy Spirit has promised to convict the hearers of the truth as we present it to them.

● *Unity*. We have seen that criticism and pride divide the fellowship and destroy the unity of the body of Christ. The answer to division is unity! Christians are called upon to maintain the unity of the Spirit in the bond of peace. That is the weapon to wield against Satan.

● *The Name of Jesus*. All the criticism that Paul faced was inspired by selfishness. But Paul was not worried about himself and his reputation. Rather, he was anxious for the honour and glory of Jesus. He was set on upholding the Name of Jesus. When temptation came to him, it was 'in the Name of Jesus' that he resisted it. When he prayed for others he found authority in 'the Name of Jesus' to ask for healing, blessing or freedom from evil spirits. When he had to face hardship and mounting pressure it was 'in the Name of Jesus' – and for Jesus' sake – rather than in the strength of his own name, that he carried on.

Prayer, praise, love, truth, unity and the Name of Jesus are not the weapons that the world uses to get its way. Nor are they a complete list of the weapons available (see, for example Ephesians 6:10–20). But they are the weapons that Paul would have used to win the spiritual battles that he faced.

So, how does this work out for us today?

Your boss rushes into work late on a Monday morning after a bad weekend. He accuses you of not getting work done – which he had actually forgotten to ask you to do. How do you react?

Your natural reaction might be to hit back, perhaps making a sarcastic comment about not being a mind-reader, and it would be nice to be told what work was expected of you. Far better to ask the Lord to help you look at things first from your boss's perspective, to give you his love for him, and to help you respond gently, though truthfully, about the situation.

You discover that people are spreading rumours and lies about you in the church. How should you react? Leave the church? Spread counter-rumours to get your own back? Have a word privately with the people concerned so that the unity of the fellowship can be restored?

Satan whispers to you that God isn't hearing your prayers for your children. He claims that it's your fault that your children aren't Christians. How do you react? Panic or praise Jesus for who he is and for all that he can do? Feel dejected, or rejoice that you belong to Jesus, and that he is working his purposes out for your family?

Have right ambitions

It is 'every man for himself' in some places. 'Look after number one' is the slogan on the young man's tee-shirt. 'Me first' is the attitude of the husband ordering his wife and children about as he gets ready for work in the morning. Not so with Paul. He has faced the selfish ambition of the Corinthians. He has resisted the devious attacks of Satan. He has seen the false apostles intent on keeping their names before the world. Paul's ambitions were very different.

The growth of the church

> 'For even if I boast somewhat freely about the
> authority the Lord gave us for building you up
> rather than pulling you down, I will not be ashamed
> of it.' *2 Corinthians 10:8*

Paul is jealous for the church in Corinth as a man is jealous for his bride. He longs for what is best for her. Despite the way the Corinthians had treated him, Paul continually has their best interests at heart. He wants only to build them up, encourage and strengthen them.

He visited the church three times. The first visit (Acts 18) was the *pioneer* visit when the church was established through months of faithful preaching and teaching. Paul worked hard and slept little, not for his benefit but for the blessing of the people at Corinth.

There was the second *painful* visit (2 Corinthians 2:5 and 7:12) when Paul had to discipline the church and be severe with one of its members. Again, he wasn't doing this for his own benefit, but to restore the holiness and happiness of the Church.

There would be the third *pastoral* visit (2 Corinthians 13:1). Paul wanted to see them again in order to encourage them in their Christian lives.

Two things especially encourage me – and probably most Christians. First, the unexpected word of appreciation for something I've done, or the person I may be. Secondly, the card or letter out of the blue when the writer tells me that God urged them to pray for me on a particular date. I know I'm not forgotten either by the Lord or by my fellow Christians. As members of the body of Christ our task is to encourage and exhort one another.

The spread of the gospel

> 'Our hope is that, as your faith continues to grow,
> our area of activity among you will greatly expand, so
> that we can preach the gospel in the regions beyond
> you.'   *2 Corinthians 10:15–16*

Paul makes it very clear that he longs to preach the gospel in the areas beyond Corinth. And in his letter to the Romans he wrote: 'It has always been my ambition to preach the gospel where Christ was not known.'

This should also be our ambition. It is easy to give our energies to evangelism where someone else has already done the hard ground-work. Paul deliberately avoided doing that, partly because the needs elsewhere were so great, and partly to avoid the rivalry that could, as we have seen, so easily spring up between evangelists.

There are many places within reach of us, where Christ is not yet known. For example:

The children of our country. Unless the children hear the gospel at church, school or home, they will grow up ignorant of Jesus. A few hear it at school, a few hear it at church. But a frightening proportion of children in our schools today simply haven't a clue who 'Jesus' is. There are things you can do to improve the situation:

• We can do what a growing number of churches have done, which is to set up a school-support group at church to pray for the local schools, the staff and the children. Christian parents from the same school might meet together for prayer. In our own church, a retired teacher compiles a termly prayer list of all the teachers in the congregation.

• It is possible to offer help with assemblies or with

Religious Studies periods. The organisation, *Christians in Education*, now part of *Care* Trust, will be able to give you help on how to go about this.

● We can suggest that our church runs a holiday club geared particularly for children who do not yet come to church.

● We can give financial help to make it possible to run a mission among children in our area, or to finance a local full-time Christian worker in schools for a county or borough.

● We can pray more regularly for our God-children, nephews and nieces, and make the effort to find out what things they are finding particularly tough and would like you to pray about.

● We can offer to help with a summer beach mission or camp – as a group leader, cook, general handyman, or anything else that is needed.

Europe. Many of us visit France, Germany or other European countries for our holidays. Some areas are largely devoid of the knowledge of Jesus. Are there steps we can take to make Christ known in Europe? Let me suggest the following:

● When you travel to the continent, take some simple Christian leaflets produced in the language of the country you are visiting. Your local Christian bookshop may well stock such leaflets, alternatively you can obtain them from Christian Literature Crusade bookshops or the Scripture Gift Mission.

● Put that area of Europe on your heart and on your prayer list before you go. Get to know the country and something of the language, and keep in touch with what is happening there. If you travel frequently in Europe on business, you may have the opportunity to build up links with particular churches and foster relationships with specific individuals whom you meet on a regular basis.

● You could suggest that your church begins to think and pray more seriously about the spread of the gospel in Europe. Perhaps your church could 'twin' with a similar church in France or Germany, and give them support and encouragement.

● Invite fellow Christians you know in other countries to visit you. Perhaps this might result in their asking a team from your church to return the visit.

Our friends and neighbours. You might be surprised to discover how little your non-Christian friends and neighbours actually know about Jesus. Here you could:

● Think of three people you know well and whom you long to know Jesus. Write their names down on a piece of paper, keep that list in your Bible and begin to pray that their minds might be open to the truth of the gospel.

● If you can, find two other people who want to do the same thing and form a 'prayer triplet' to pray together.

In these ways you will be using spiritual weapons on behalf of those friends, fulfilling a God-given ambition and beginning to find a fruitful, rather than a frustrated, life.

Paul exchanged the pressure of criticism for the greater pressure of making Christ known.

The glory of Christ
Paul's parting shot to his critics is:

'Let him who boasts, boast in the Lord. For it is not

123

the man who commends himself who is approved,
but the man whom the Lord commends.'

2 Corinthians 10:17–18

I suspect Paul would have been good at judo. The technique in judo, so I'm told, is to so use the weight of your opponent's attack that your opponent is thrown by it himself. That is exactly what Paul does here! Instead of being broken by criticism, he robbed it of its power by turning it back on itself. Paul used the accusations levelled at him to point to the graciousness and greatness of Christ – it is *Christ's* commendation that really counts.

When we are criticised, for whatever reason, we need to look for ways of turning it to God's glory. This will mean letting the experience teach us to become stronger, and to rely even more fully on Christ.

If the charges are true, we must of course accept them and, for the sake of Christ, we must try to learn from them. But if the charges are false, we shall do well to respond as Paul did – with silence or with bold reaffirmation of the truth.

8

PRESSURE
THAT NEVER
LETS UP

'Stress forces Dalglish to leave Liverpool', ran the headline on my morning paper on 23 February 1991. 'Kenny Dalglish resigned as Manager of Liverpool yesterday. The pressure of six years running Britain's most successful soccer club had become too much.'

'Stress' is a word about which we hear a lot. Christians are not free from it, nor from those factors that produce it. And many people make a living out of treating it!

It's fascinating to compare Kenny Dalglish's position with that of one of our Church members working in Buenos Aires, South America. The city's name literally means 'Beautiful Air'. The daily reality is very different. In a letter home to us at All Saints', Judy wrote,

'What's happening in Argentina? In December there was another attempted military coup. (It was a strange sensation to be watching the news "live" on television, and simultaneously hear the gunfire from my window.) Social unrest is bubbling. A court case is exposing corruption at the highest levels of the political and judicial system; inflation was twenty-seven percent last month; the teachers are on strike so most schools didn't start the year (it's impossible to live on a teacher's salary); the trains are on strike, causing chaos and misery for the millions who travel long hours daily as it is; and the cholera epidemic has reached Argentina, causing the northern and western borders to be closed.'

Paul, too, knew extreme and constant stress:

'Are they Hebrews? So am I. Are they Israelites? So am I. Are they Abraham's descendants? So am I. Are they servants of Christ? (I am out of my mind to talk like this.) I am more. I have worked much harder, been in prison more frequently, been flogged more severely, and been exposed to death again and again. Five times I received from the Jews the forty lashes minus one. Three times I was beaten with rods, once I was stoned, three times I was shipwrecked, I spent a night and a day in the open sea, I have been constantly on the move. I have been in danger from rivers, in danger from bandits, in danger from my own countrymen, in danger from Gentiles, in danger in the city, in danger in the country, in danger at sea; and in danger from false brothers. I have laboured and toiled and have often gone without sleep; I have known hunger and thirst and have often gone without food; I have been cold and naked. Besides everything else, I face daily the pressure of my concern for all the churches. Who is weak, and I do not feel weak? Who is led into sin, and I do not inwardly burn?

If I must boast, I will boast of the things that show my weakness. The God and Father of the Lord Jesus, who is to be praised for ever, knows that I am not lying. In Damascus the governor under King

Aretas had the city of the Damascenes guarded in order to arrest me. But I was lowered in a basket from a window in the wall and slipped through his hands.'
2 Corinthians 11:22–33

That's an overwhelming list! I've always assumed that it is a unique list, but now I'm not sure. Such events happen to other people as well. For instance, take Bishop Alan's letter which arrived recently from Peru. It was almost as if I was reading a modern account of 2 Corinthians:

'We settled back here quickly and easily again, thanks to all those who were praying for us especially at that time but, sadly, things in Peru were in a worse state than when we left.

The Ministry of Health's official figures for cholera are over 157,000 registered cases, of which more than 1,100 have died. The actual numbers could be quite a lot higher than that, as many of the poorer folk in Lima cannot afford doctor's fees or medicines, and in the remote areas of Peru there are virtually no medical facilities anyway.

On April 4th and 5th the high jungle region of Alto Mayo was hit by two earthquakes. Thirty-four people were killed, and 290 injured. The experts say that there have been 400 tremors since – Lima has had three quite noticeable ones – and more are threatened. Relief was slow in reaching the jungle because of bad weather and lack of available aircraft.

The same night, Lima's electricity was cut off as Sendero Luminoso [Shining Path] terrorists again blew up a number of electricity pylons (despite their being protected by anti-personnel mines). During the blackout, a well co-ordinated attack was carried out against twenty-two banks and five embassies, including the British. Things have long been difficult in the Andean areas, with comments like the following appearing almost daily in the newspapers:

"The Mayor of Huamanga, along with the Governor and Lieutenant Governor of San Pedro do Cachi, Ayaucho, were shot dead when a group of Sendero Luminoso terrorists entered the town."

"Thirteen villagers were reported to have died in yet another massacre by Sendero Luminoso."

"Twenty-three members of the local Civil Defence Group, including women and children, were brutally massacred by Sendero Luminoso on Saturday night, for refusing to carry out subversive commands."

This week the terrorists have been especially busy in Lima, with around seventy-five incidents in the last four days. The nearest to us was a car-bomb (an estimated thirty kilos of dynamite) about half a mile from our house. Thankfully, no-one was killed, and very few people injured, despite damage to buildings, and countless windows of local flats and houses being blown in.

Seasonal heavy rains have caused havoc and several villages have been wiped out by mudslides. Lima's water supply was affected by accumulated garbage in the River Rimac (which at the best of times is absolutely filthy!!).

Peru is the country with the highest number of people reported missing, or disappeared, according to the UN Human Rights Commission which met in Geneva in March. We live under a permanent State of Emergency.'

Then I read a letter from Archbishop George Browne

from Liberia in West Africa, who had written to reassure those who were anxious about his personal safety during the violence and civil war which broke out in his country. He wrote:

> 'In spite of the fact that Liberian religious leaders were a target, not one of us who remained in the country was killed. God sheltered us and death passed over us. Obviously, the price was high: arrests, humiliation, threats, harassment, dispossession of assets, and food shortages.
>
> This ordeal left its toll on our bodies. I lost some forty pounds in weight and had to reduce my clerical collar size from 16 to 14.
>
> Satan obtained permission to test the faith of Liberians, but he did not triumph. Your prayers helped to sustain us.'

Stress hits hard in the UK as well. 'It is thirty years since the first shocks of the permissive society hit the United Kingdom', so we were told recently by *Care* magazine. The magazine spelt out the details:

> 'Every day 420 children experience their parents' divorce and one-third of those children are under five. Thirty-three percent of children lose touch with one parent after divorce.
>
> Although the overwhelming majority (eighty-three percent) of married or cohabiting couples expect life long partnership, only thirty-seven percent attain it. Thirty-seven percent of single parents are single women who have never married. A quarter of all babies are born out of wedlock. Fifty-one percent of divorced men who have not remarried wished they had stayed with their former spouse. In 1979,

185,000 single women were cohabiting. In 1987 it was 617,000.'

The pressure of daily life in today's world is a major problem. We don't need convincing there is a problem. But is there an answer to it?

We'll discover an answer by looking at two areas. First, we need to recognise the sources of our stress. Paul helps us here by being specific about the pressures that affected him. Then we need to look at what we can do to help relieve stress.

RECOGNISING THE SOURCES OF STRESS

Paul gives us an amazing catalogue of the personal and daily pressures that he faced in his ministry. We can isolate eight groups of pressures in his list – and can probably identify with many of them in our own situations.

Family expectations

Because other people were boasting of the family they came from and the people they were related to, so does Paul. He says his background and family are worth boasting about more than theirs! His religious pedigree as a Hebrew was impeccable; socially his parents had given him a head start by being Roman citizens; educationally they had fixed him up with a top-class professor at one of the most prestigious universities of his day (Acts 22:3). But family background is no shield against the pressures of daily life. Sometimes it increases them.

I write this on the day that India mourns the assassination of Rajiv Gandhi. It was hoped that he would continue the Nehru dynasty that had already ruled for forty years: his family background forced him into a particular role in life and vastly increased his daily pressures.

The Guinness family is famous for its brewing, its banking and also for its Christian members. Yet its recent history shows that fame has not protected it from great testing and daily pressure.

In day to day life, you and I may also face the pressure of having a well-known father or mother, and having to live up to the family name. Or perhaps our parents have made great sacrifices for our education and so we feel an obligation to be successful. We may have a very bright brother or sister who just coasts through exams, but we have to slog at our work to achieve anything like the same results. We can feel the pressure to match up to others in sport and social life too. In all these situations we need to recognise that we are under these pressures, and make sure that we allow ourselves to be free to be who we really are.

Sometimes we are under pressure for the opposite reasons: perhaps people have a low expectation of us, or we have a low opinion of ourselves. Either situation is inhibiting and limits our freedom to achieve what we actually could. Or we might live in a depressed area where the 'high-flier' is a social oddity and peer-pressure to stay 'normal' begins to influence the choices we make in life.

Stress from serving others

Sometimes people assume that those who work in 'full-time' ministry as clergy, pastors or missionaries are free from pressures. 'You don't have to travel into London each day,' I'm reminded occasionally. 'You have a secure job . . . a house is provided . . . you just don't know what *real* pressure is!'

It's true that I don't experience pressure at those exact points, but I do have to deal with other pressures. For one thing, I'm constantly on the job. I can't relax unless I'm physically 'off site' – which means I can never relax at home! No Christian work is a mere forty-hour week: I'm dealing constantly with an infinite variety of demands. I am expected to cope with the hopes and expectations, the fears and criticisms of a host of people. There is daily pressure for the servant of Christ.

Most mothers know the pressure of constantly caring for their families – washing, ironing, shopping, cooking, listening to their children's problems and complaints. This is made more difficult if Mum has to have a paid job too. Many a mum has felt an unpaid and unappreciated slave to her family, frequently near tears of frustration.

Physical suffering and fear of abuse

Some of the beatings, imprisonments and floggings suffered by Paul are recorded specifically in Acts. We once spent a holiday at Paphos in Cyprus, where Paul had been. Near to the little church used by the Anglican Chaplaincy at Paphos is 'Paul's Pillar' where he was once bound and whipped thirty-nine times for his preaching of Jesus Christ.

We have stood in the 25,000-seater theatre at Ephesus, and imagined the uproar that surrounded Paul's visit there. You can look across to the caves beneath the huge stadium where hungry lions would have been chained, ready to be set loose on anyone who lost favour with the authorities.

Paul's suffering and abuse were often at the hands of the authorities. Many people today are in daily fear of their safety from those 'in authority' over them – be that a violent husband, abusive parents or a manipulative employer. There are elderly parents who feel 'a nuisance' to short-tempered and busy adult children. A recent report from a thirty-eight year old nurse is both fascinating and disturbing. She disguised herself as an old woman in order to experience what it was like to be old in the community. She noted the sort of treatment she got at the supermarket check-out, at the doctors, on the bus and crossing the road, and discovered just how unkind we can be as a nation to older people.

People of a different race, colour or faith are also very aware of abuse, prejudice and seeming discrimination, making it necessary for local authorities to employ race relations officers to promote more harmonious community relationships.

Others feel disadvantaged by 'the system' itself. Some of the items in Esther Rantzen's TV programme, *That's Life*, reveal people who have been misunderstood and face increasing frustration from apparently incompetent local officials who are 'just doing their job'.

Daily dangers

Some friends of ours in a Muslim country wrote asking for prayer. Hostile bandits were operating in the small village where they worked. This couple had an eighteen-year old daughter who had to travel from the village each day for her studies. Would we please pray for her daily protection, they asked.

Paul lived in a dangerous world; so do we, to some extent. The older member who wants to get to the evening service at church is afraid of coming out after dark. People living in inner city areas may know what it is to fear attack in broad daylight. Parents live with the stress of wondering how safe their child will be as he cycles to school on busy roads. Commuters on the train into London wonder if there will be another bomb alert this morning. Many people's jobs take them into potentially dangerous situations – a construction site, a coal mine, a nuclear processing plant. Our daily awareness of potential danger can leave us stressed, anxious and irritable.

Lack of basic necessities

Sometimes Paul went without sleep, food or drink. Almost certainly this was not by choice. It was a compulsory fast. We may well choose to go without sleep or food in order to get work completed, or to gain some spiritual advantage. But that is not always the case. People in some of our cities – and in some country areas – lack adequate housing. The places they live in are dilapidated, damp and inadequately heated. They suffer the deprivation of basic necessities. Others find that their unemployment pay or family income supplement just doesn't go far enough. A daughter may spend restless nights on the sofa, watching over a dying relative, or a mother is constantly up in the night nursing a sick child. Whatever the basic necessity is of which we are deprived – decent living conditions, finance or sleep – we will suffer stress as a result.

Work pressures

'Besides everything else,' says Paul – and I feel it is a masterly understatement! – 'I face daily the pressure of my concern for all the churches.' Paul's work is sometimes in danger of getting on top of him.

One of the reasons we look forward to holidays is that they set us free for a little while from this daily pressure. Each of us will have different pressures, and every job brings some. There are last-minute orders to be despatched, deadlines to meet, unreasonable expectations from our bosses. There is the threat of redundancy, the hurt of receiving yet more rejection letters, or the sheer build-up of tiredness, worry and sleepless nights, making us less and less able to cope with each successive day.

Identifying with the stresses of others

Paul identifies with the suffering of others – either in their weakness or in their temptations.

Our concern for other people can cause us stress and pressure on their behalf. We try to put ourselves in the other person's position, and feel helpless to do anything. We want to help, but we can't. We long to visit that person in hospital, but we can't be in two places at once. We would love to give a friend some help with redecorating their front room, but we are expected to visit some relatives. All these different situations bring pressure on those who care.

And there are thousands of 'carers' in the world. They care in a sacrificial way, with unflagging love, for someone in need. As a result, they don't get time to themselves. They can't get to church or to a fellowship group; their social life is non-existent. They feel isolated, forgotten and neglected, taken for granted. They are people bearing daily pressure.

The pressure of unexpected events

Paul ends his list with one specific event which seems rather trivial. He was let down from a window in the city wall of Damascus, in a basket. The king had set a guard on the city to make sure that Paul didn't escape, but his friends ensured that he did! What can we learn from this event?

First, pressure may come in small or unexpected ways. We are having a quiet evening at home when the phone rings. It's a call that we find upsetting and we are restless and upset for the rest of the evening. A minor happening like that can cloud a whole day.

Secondly, it was unexpected. Paul suddenly heard of the plot to capture him and his plans were immediately thrown to the wind in order to cope with this emergency. Any sudden crisis throws our known world and regular routines into disarray – and so causes us stress.

Thirdly, that story reminds us that Paul was weak and vulnerable; he was willing and ready to admit it. Other people would have to lower him through the window. He needed help and support in times of pressure and weakness. We know it can be stressful to have to admit to needing help from others, but perhaps many of us are under greater pressure because we fail to admit our need.

DEALING WITH STRESS

We can seek help today for stress from a growing number of professional bodies and people. In addition to the family doctor, there are stress clinics, physiotherapists, psychotherapists and counsellors, together with a variety of drugs and other helps. But there are also two key things we can do to help ourselves.

Recognise the symptoms

It is important to learn to recognise the 'tell-tale' signals of stress in our lives. Take note if you find yourself thinking or feeling things like: 'I find it hard to cope; I get ratty with the family; I feel exhausted; I never get a good night's sleep; I don't enjoy doing things; I want to run and hide; I can't concentrate; I find it hard to make up my mind; I find I'm forgetting things these days; I can't get my breath easily; I find myself comfort-eating.' These are just a few of the stress indicators to watch out for.

In addition, be aware that any change in life's circumstances, whether expected or not, will produce stress. Different people will find they react to similar events in different ways, but among the most obviously stressful changes are the death of a spouse, divorce, marital separation, the death of a close family member, personal injury or illness and a change of job. At the other end of the scale – though still causing stress – are such minor events as a change in sleeping habits, a family get-together, and holidays!

In between will come all the other changes in life – such as taking out a mortgage, beginning or ending school, trouble at work, or moving house.

It is clear that none of us is going to be free from stressful circumstances in life.

Develop coping strategies

Stress comes when pressure is put on one part of my life so that the balance of life is upset. To cope with this, then, I need to re-balance my life. This may mean that I need to look after my physical needs by eating more wisely or taking more exercise. I may need to carve out more 'space' for myself in my daily programme, or develop new interests and hobbies. I may need to cut down on the amount of work I do, and have more time with my family and friends.

It is important to make sure that the priorities we want in life are the ones that actually operate. For example, what priorities do you *want* to give to the following, and what do you *actually* give them: your work, spouse, children, faith, your own personal interests, your parents, your 'good works'? How does your answer compare with the Christian teaching that suggests the right order of priorities should be: God, our spouse, children, other family, work, church activities?

Professional studies have shown that those who believe in themselves and what they are doing will be able to cope well with stress. But those who have a poor self-image or inferiority complex, will be far more vulnerable to the stresses of life.

We need to identify the points and causes of stress, and re-organise our patterns of life accordingly.

Get professional help

A great deal of professional, practical and medical help

is available for those suffering stress. We should not regard such help as an alternative to, or in conflict with, the spiritual help that may also be available. We are whole people with bodies, minds, spirits, and emotions. Each part of us will affect the well-being of every other part of us: a depressed mind will affect our body; a sick body will affect our emotions.

The Lord wants us to be whole people. To achieve this we sometimes need physical help, sometimes emotional help, sometimes spiritual help. The different means of help do not conflict with each other, but are complementary.

If you feel unable to cope with the stress you are under at present, why not consider one of the following courses of action?

• Talk over your personal circumstances and problems with a trusted Christian friend who will listen and pray with you.
• Make an appointment to discuss the situation with your vicar, pastor or minister. He may be able to help directly and personally, or he may feel that someone other than himself is better able to help you, and might suggest some such person.
• You may wish to talk things over with your local GP.
• You could contact one of the organisations set up specifically to help people deal with stress. Details of seminars on stress prevention and management can be obtained from: Stress and Life Trust (SALT), The Istana, Freezeland Lane, Bexhill-on-Sea, East Sussex, TN39 5JD.

9

PRESSURE
THAT LEADS
TO BLESSING

'Most people can cope with one major crisis in life, but not with two.' That comment from a former warden of St George's Crypt in Leeds has remained with me for more than thirty years. I was curate at that city centre church at the time. My colleague, the warden, had observed from his ministry to many men in trouble that they could cope with losing a job, or with a divorce, or with a death in the family. Yet if more than one of these were thrown at them at the same time, the pressure would be likely to break them.

Yet multi-pressure still comes to us. Joan, for example, is bringing up a young family. She has an alcoholic husband, and he is living away from home with another woman. Joan has just been diagnosed as having breast cancer. Yet she has a faith, is supported by the prayers of her Christian friends, and is seeing God at work in her family.

The same is true of Yvonne. John, her husband, is not sure whether his job is secure during the recession. Peter, their son, is regularly playing truant from school. At midnight they may not know where he is, and they are also having to care for a dying mother. Yet, I usually find a smile on Yvonne's face and a sense of joy in her heart. Humanly speaking I wonder how she has been able to keep going.

We have looked at a variety of pressures, as they appear both in Paul's life and in ours, and have discovered some ways of dealing with them. But now we find that, strange as it may seem, Paul also says that pressures can bring blessing:

> 'I must go on boasting. Although there is nothing to be gained, I will go on to visions and revelations from the Lord. I know a man in Christ who fourteen years ago was caught up to the third heaven. Whether it was in the body or out of the body I do not know – God knows. And I know that this man – whether in the body or apart from the body I do not know, but God knows – was caught up to paradise. He heard inexpressible things, things that man is not permitted to tell. I will boast about a man like that, but I will not boast about myself, except about my weaknesses. Even if I should choose to boast, I would not be a fool, because I would be speaking the truth. But I refrain, so no-one will think more of me than is warranted by what I do or say.'   *2 Corinthians 12:1–6*

THE BLESSING OF A POWERFUL TESTIMONY

Although he refers to 'a man in Christ,' Paul is really giving his own personal testimony. He speaks about a specially vivid and intense revelation that the Lord gave him about fourteen years previously.

Visions had played a part in Paul's life before. Sometimes God had shown him the next part of his missionary plan. At other times God had encouraged him when he was feeling depressed. In this particular vision Paul found himself in paradise. The word had originally been used of a Persian walled garden that belonged to the king. Perhaps Paul is saying that he found himself walking and talking – whether physically or spiritually – in a 'garden' with the King of kings – the Lord himself.

Paul is not hankering for the past and the good old days. Nor is he bemoaning the fact that his spiritual life is not what it used to be. Rather, he is drawing strength for himself from that special occasion as he presses on day by day. Testimony – the story of what the Lord has done in our lives or other people's – is powerful.

Paul often used his testimony as a means of sharing the good news of Jesus. The early church gave testimony to the fact that Jesus was risen from the dead. Testimony is also a weapon to use against the devil when he tries to discourage us and depress us about the potential of any given situation. For example, a number of Christian parents battle with the pressure of their children spending too much time and money in the local pubs. Despite their past Christian teaching, these young people choose at this moment to sit light to the Christian faith.

How easy it is to be discouraged in that situation! 'What did we do wrong?' ask the parents. 'Where did I fail as a father?' asks Dad. 'Will they grow up as alcoholics?' wonders someone else. Blessing arises in the midst of these pressures when such Christians are able to remember how God has answered prayer in the past, particularly when they can see positive changes that have already come about in their children's lives.

So it is wise to look back, from time to time, to

see how God has answered our prayers at such times. We will be reminded of how God helped in that crisis and we'll see what progress has been made since, and this will be ammunition for us that we can store up for coping with the next attack. Faith will grow. We will be discovering blessings even in the midst of stress.

THE BLESSING OF WEAKNESS

But we know it's not always as straightforward as that. Life isn't a bed of roses, because even roses have thorns! We sometimes struggle to achieve something, only to be constantly defeated by our own weaknesses. That can be depressing!

> 'To keep me from becoming conceited because of these surpassingly great revelations, there was given me a thorn in my flesh, a messenger of Satan, to torment me. Three times I pleaded with the Lord to take it away from me, but he said to me, "My grace is sufficient for you, for my power is made perfect in weakness." Therefore I will boast all the more gladly about my weaknesses, so that Christ's power may rest on me.'   *2 Corinthians 12:7–9*

Paul knew not only great revelations, but also severe restrictions. The 'thorn' he speaks of is not one from a rose bush, but rather more of a fence stake! It's more like a spear or a fish hook, or the stake on which a man would be crucified. Paul also describes this as 'a messenger of Satan.' He felt it was destructive, crippling, hampering to his ministry.

Paul realised that Satan's power was limited, and that Satan had no power except that allowed him by

God. So the natural thing was to pray that God would remove this 'thorn in the flesh'. Three times Paul prayed, and three times God said 'No'.

We are not sure what the problem was. Three possibilities have been suggested:

● *A particular vulnerability to temptation.* Paul's spiritual 'Achilles heel' that Satan always attacked. Most Christians have areas in their lives where they are more vulnerable to temptation than others. Paul could be suggesting that Satan was constantly attacking those areas of weakness.

● *A physical ailment.* A second view is that Paul might have suffered from poor eyesight or from splitting headaches and migraine. Those who have suffered these will know how debilitating they can be. Others have suggested that Paul was an epileptic, or had attacks of fever. We do know that Paul had poor eyesight because in one letter he speaks about the size of his handwriting.

● *Opposition.* The third commonly-suggested meaning relates the 'thorn' to those people who resisted the work God had given Paul to do. He felt their opposition like thorns pricking him, painfully.

Most areas of Christian work are attacked in this sort of way. One or two key people seem set on opposing what the leadership is planning. Or there is one person in the fellowship group who grabs the limelight and dominates the running of the group. Or there is a member of staff at the local school who always criticises us. It only takes one member of the family to make life a real struggle.

The experience of God's grace

Just as Jesus prayed three times in the Garden of Gethsemane that God would remove the cup of suffering (Matthew 26:36–46) and God said 'No', so Paul prayed three times that God would remove this thing that was debilitating his ministry, and God said 'No'. But at the same time, God also gave Paul a marvellous promise: 'My grace is sufficient for you.'

Prebendary Webb-Peplow was a great Christian leader and speaker at the Keswick Convention. He was vicar of a fashionable London church. But his three-year-old daughter died. He was devastated. He couldn't work, and he couldn't find any comfort.

On his study wall hung that text: 'My grace is sufficient for you.' Looking up at it one afternoon he realised that the word 'IS' had been written in capital letters. In the midst of his sadness and the pressure of death, God brought him the assurance that he would pull through; God's grace really was and would be sufficient for his need.

When Paul says that God's grace is available, he uses a word that means 'continually available'. The shop that boasts it is 'able to meet all your needs' is not telling the truth! Sometimes it's shut! And even if it's open, the thing you want might be out of stock. Not so with the grace and power of God. They are constantly in stock, and God is 'open *all* hours'.

The comedian, Ken Dodd, interviewed by Dr Anthony Clare shortly after his trial for alleged tax evasion, commented, 'In desperation you try to make bargains. But if you knock on a door and nobody answers you tend to think there is nobody at home. I say this without embarrassment at all. The power of prayer was a wonderful thing to discover anew. I would recommend it to anyone who has a problem. Don't be afraid to get in touch with head office' (*Daily Telegraph*, 20 September, 1990).

Sarah Jones is a nursing sister at one of our London Teaching Hospitals. An accident she sustained as a fifteen year-old, playing hockey, went undetected for some time. Now it has brought problems and she has been off work for more than two years because of it. She has undergone seven major operations for the rebuilding of her knee, and knows intense pain. Yet she is continuing to trust and rejoice in the Lord.

Tom, together with Nancy his American wife, were full-time Christian workers. Tom was diagnosed as having cancer. Prayer was offered for him and he underwent treatment. He has been able to continue his outstanding and yet quiet Christian work of leading young men and women to a faith in Christ in almost every European country. Fellowships have been established as a result of his work. Tom's weakness could have led him to pack up and go back to the States; instead, in his weakness, he and Nancy discovered more of the grace of God, and have been able to enjoy the spiritual fruit that has resulted.

A young Christian man was trapped in Kuwait at the outbreak of the war with Iraq in September 1990. Writing home to his parents he said,

'There are road blocks everywhere. Escape across the desert borders seems unlikely. No doubt there are minefields and other nasties also. I thought about a long night walk at the time of the last full moon, but staying put always seemed the best option.

I have found that my faith has helped a great

deal in this situation and have found Psalms 46 and 97 particularly uplifting, along with Romans 8.

I am sure that, in a mysterious way, all this trouble is part of God's sovereign plan, and that a great deal of good will come out of it in the end. Remember that he is "Lord of Hosts", Jehovah Sabaoth, The God of Armies, and he can use all men and things to his purpose.'

The experience of God's power

'That is why, for Christ's sake, I delight in weaknesses, in insults, in hardships, in persecutions, in difficulties. For when I am weak, then I am strong.'   *2 Corinthians 12:10*

Paul had discovered that his own strength couldn't achieve very much, but that God's could. And when his own strength wasn't in the way, that is, when he felt really weak, God could work through far more effectively.

I learned this truth from my successor at St Thomas' Church, Crookes, in Sheffield. In 1970 we left a church of about 150 people. Twenty years later that church had grown to 1250! When I asked Canon Robert Warren what his next task was he replied, 'How the church can grow from 1250 to 1500'!

The story of that growth has been written in *In the Crucible*. But the story behind the headlines has been described in *On the Anvil* (both published by Highland Books, 1988 and 1990). In his second book Robert Warren describes how he learned to lead such a work:

'My conviction, which has arisen both from the study

of scripture and from reflection on my own experience, is that, for the Christian, learning takes place at the point of weakness. Pain, failure and change are at the heart of Christian learning; blessing, success and achievement are simply the fruit of that learning process.

For most of us, the process of finding God's power at work out of weakness, and his life rising up out of our 'deaths', is a slow one. At times we will feel that nothing is happening. Things are just as they have always been. We shall need to be patient. But gradually we shall realise that God is at work, and that our circumstances are changing.

It is hard to bear this waiting alone. Why not share the problem with a few close Christian friends so that they can pray with you, encourage you, and rejoice with you when you find that God is answering prayer?

Sam and Belinda both came from unhappy family backgrounds. Sam never knew who his parents were. He was fostered out as a young lad, and never felt he was accepted in that home. As soon as he could he left school, and the family. He found 'digs' and a job. Yet all the time he was not sure where he 'belonged'; he found it hard to trust people; he felt he was always being criticised. Then he met Belinda.

They now have a young daughter and a pleasant home. They both have good jobs, but underneath there is still weakness. Belinda was abused by her father when he had had too much to drink, and she carries the emotional scars of that relationship to this day. Sam and Belinda love and care for each other deeply. But they also aggravate each other's past weaknesses, and need great help to heal the hurts of the past. Power is coming into those fragile areas, but it is a slow and painful experience. When they feel defeated they hang on to those words, 'My power is made perfect in your weakness'.

A husband, sad but proud, sat in his daughter's house. The wife to whom he had been married for many years had died suddenly. He wasn't sure where to turn for help in his weakness. Then he was shown a copy of our monthly church magazine in which someone had put the following prayer. Later, he told me he prayed it again and again. Through turning in prayer to the Lord in his weakness, he began to find the grace and power that he so desperately needed:

A Prayer to Jesus, our Saviour

Lord, hold my hand,
   I so need your loving kindness;

Lord, hold my hand,
   all through life, in joy or grief.

Lord, hold my hand,
   when I'm sick with fear and anxious;

Lord, hold my hand,
   In the wonder of relief.

Lord, hold my hand,
   When it's dark and storms are raging;

Lord, hold my hand,
   and help me live it through.

Lord, hold my hand,
   When I'm lifted, joyful, loving;

Lord, hold my hand,
   When I'm trying something new.

Lord, hold my hand,
 When I fail or faint or waver;

Lord, hold my hand,
 For I know your love is true.

Lord, hold my hand,
 When I'm lonely, weary, ageing;

Lord, hold my hand,
 When there's only me – and You.

                        Amen.

10

GOD'S CONTINUING HELP

The morning routine includes taking the milk in, and dealing with the post. Fortunately, not all the post is for me! Some letters are short and to the point. Sometimes there will be a very long letter – pages and pages of it. I wade through, waiting for the writer to get to the point. Why has he written?

It's the same with Paul. When we get almost to the end of his letter to the Corinthians he tells them why he wrote it:

> 'This is why I write these things when I am absent, that when I come I may not have to be harsh in my use of authority – the authority the Lord gave me for building you up, not for tearing you down.'
>
> *2 Corinthians 13:10*

As we have seen, things were wrong in the church and Paul was under pressure to put them right. He was also under pressure from his opponents and, while needing to respond to them, was under pressure to preach the gospel in other parts of Asia Minor. He also longs to get the collection for the Christians at Jerusalem completed.

Pressures from the past, pressures in the present and the pressure of the future! Yet in all these situations he wants the Corinthians to be sure of God's continuing help.

PRESSURES OF THE PAST, PRESENT AND FUTURE

Paul summarises what has been wrong, so far as the past is concerned: proper disciplinary measures had not been taken against a particular member of the congregation. He had to warn the church that this sin would have to be judged and punished, and advised the fellowship to deal with it themselves. And he gave them a strong warning: if they failed to do so, Paul would visit them and deal with the situation personally:

> 'This will be my third visit to you. "Every matter must be established by the testimony of two or three witnesses." I already gave you a warning when I was with you the second time. I now repeat it while absent: On my return I will not spare those who sinned earlier or any of the others, since you are demanding proof that Christ is speaking through me. He is not weak in dealing with you, but is powerful among you.'   *2 Corinthians 13:1–3*

Paul is concerned to deal not only with what has been wrong in the past, but to ensure that they won't fail again in the future. So he sets them a 'test' for the present: are they really living in the faith, walking closely with Jesus Christ? And are they accepting the teaching of God's word in their lives as their guide to what is true and right?

'Examine yourselves to see whether you are in the
faith; test yourselves. Do you not realise that Christ
Jesus is in you – unless, of course, you fail the test?
And I trust that you will discover that we have not
failed the test. Now we pray to God that you will
not do anything wrong. Not that people will see
that we have stood the test but that you will do what
is right even though we may seem to have failed.
For we cannot do anything against the truth, but only
for the truth. We are glad whenever we are weak
but you are strong, and our prayer is for your
perfection.'   *2 Corinthians 13:5–9*

These are searching questions for them, and for us. The
Bible is still our guide into right thinking and right
living. As we live according to the truth, so we stay
walking closely with Jesus.

'Finally, brothers, good-bye. Aim for perfection,
listen to my appeal, be of one mind, live in peace.
And the God of love and peace will be with you.
    Greet one another with a holy kiss. All the saints
send their greetings.'   *2 Corinthians 13:11–13*

It was typical of Paul to throw out some short, but
profound, last words: 'Aim for perfection'! It would
have been wrong to set any lower standard. 'Live in
peace' and 'Be of one mind' got to the heart of the
problem – they had been pulling each other to pieces!
And instead of cursing each other, Paul suggests, try 'a
holy' greeting – a kiss all round in the fellowship, a
sign of love, greeting and respect towards one another.

HELP WITH THE PAST, PRESENT AND FUTURE

Until we die, or the Lord returns, we shall go on facing the pressures of life. This is because we shall go on having to deal with the pressures of the world, the flesh and the devil.

We have constantly bumped into these three characters at Corinth. Criticism, rivalry and worldly ambitions and attitudes came from the world and from the Corinthians themselves. They were also aware that Satan was actively attacking the minds of unbelievers as well as young Christians. He was seeking to deceive and to discourage leaders and disciples alike. But the letter ends with a marvellous three-fold answer to these three sources of pressure. When we are under pressure from the world, the flesh or the devil, God's constant help is available to us in the Trinity – Father, Son and Holy Spirit. It is summed up for us in the words of 'The Grace':

> 'May the grace of the Lord Jesus Christ, and the love of God, and the fellowship of the Holy Spirit be with you all.' *2 Corinthians 13:14*

This is probably the best-known prayer, after the Lord's Prayer. You have probably said it many times. I have said it standing or sitting, formally and with deep meaning, with eyes shut, or looking around at everyone present. 'The Grace' is the summary of all the help that is available to us to deal with the pressures that face us today.

If Christian lives are like houses struck by the cold winds of criticism and the storms of sudden crises, then 'The Grace' is the foundation on which those houses should be firmly built. We have the Love of God the

Father, the Grace of the Lord Jesus Christ, and the Fellowship of the Holy Spirit: all the resources we need.

The love of God

God's love has been like a ribbon threaded all the way through this letter:

- God's love called Paul to his task of working at Corinth (1:1).
- God's love comforted him, when Paul felt completely overwhelmed (1:22–23).
- God's love helped him to stand firm in the faith when he was tempted to wobble and fall away (1:21 and 2:1).
- God's love and mercy kept him going when he was hard pressed and wanting to give up (4:1 and 4:16).
- God's love provided Paul's message of reconciliation for a world divided and falling apart (5:18).
- God's love and grace inspired Paul to urge the Corinthians to respond to that same love and grace.

God's unique covenant of love for his people assured Paul that his ministry would be successful: 'I will be their God and they shall be my people.'

The grace of the Lord Jesus

Like the love of God, the grace of Jesus figures prominently in all that Paul says. For example:

- Grace is consistent. Paul can be consistent in his plans and purposes because God is consistent. His promises can be relied on. He never says 'yes' and 'no'.

155

God's purposes don't change because God's grace does not vary (1:20).

● Grace forgives. Much criticism and many counter claims had been made at Corinth. There was a great need for forgiveness. Paul points the people to the example of Christ's forgiveness and grace as their inspiration and model (2:10).

● Grace perseveres. It was not only God's love enfolding him but his grace carrying him that helped Paul to keep going when he felt like giving in to the pressures that he faced (4:1, 16).

● Grace serves. Self-interest had played a large part in the thinking of the Corinthians and the 'super-apostles'. Paul realised, through the example of Jesus' self-giving grace, that serving others, rather than pandering to one-self, is what matters.

● Grace works to produce holiness of life. There was much sin and rebellion at Corinth. Paul knew that a proper understanding of the grace and mercy of Jesus would help them live holy lives (6:16).

● Grace gives. The remarkable thing about the Christians in Macedonia was the way they gave when they hadn't got anything! An understanding of the way Jesus continued to give inspired them to some remarkable selfless giving (8:1–5).

● Grace brings power out of weakness. The Cross of Jesus is the place where we see Christ's grace most clearly shown. It is also the place of the most dramatic transformation of weakness into power. Death gave way to life.

When we feel like being inconsistent, not forgiving others, ready to give up, wondering why we should bother to do things for other people, asking about the point of trying to live a Christlike life in an ungodly world, let us receive Jesus' grace again and so find his help to carry on.

The fellowship of the Holy Spirit

Paul also had help from the Holy Spirit – help within himself. He doesn't write a great deal about the Holy Spirit in this letter, but he says enough to assure us that we, too, have all the resources of the Spirit at our disposal.

For example:

• The Holy Spirit has marked you out as belonging to the Lord, and you have begun to receive his power. The Holy Spirit enables you to serve the Lord in ways which please him (1:22).

There are many times towards the end of a busy Sunday, when I feel I don't have the resources to cope with the pressures of a full church again that evening. I find myself coming to Jesus, admitting my need, and asking him to fill me again with his Holy Spirit. Jesus always keeps his promise. When I tell God I can't cope, he copes for me! That makes all the difference.

• The Holy Spirit gives you life (3:6). The Christian life is not a set of rules: 'Do this!' 'Don't do that!' Rather, the heart of our Christian lives is in allowing the Holy Spirit – the Spirit of Jesus – to have full control in our life. When that happens other people will see and experience something more of the Lord Jesus' presence, and we shall enjoy his life in all its fullness.

JB Phillips has translated Romans 12:1–2 as, 'Don't let the world squeeze you into its own mould.' Don't become like the people who have no time for

Jesus and who follow the standards and ways of the world. That's hard in a tough and unloving world today. But you will be able to do it as you allow the Holy Spirit to go on giving you his life and power.

● The Holy Spirit gives you freedom (3:17). Many people think that freedom is 'doing what I like'. So often that leads to boredom and bondage. Freedom is found in doing what God asks. In the midst of pressure, you can be at peace within yourself.

● The Holy Spirit makes you more like Jesus (3:18). Cars carry all sorts of wonderful slogans on their rear windows. The one I like best says, 'Don't be cross with me, Jesus hasn't finished with me yet!'

We are still rough material. The Spirit is fashioning us day by day, and little by little, to be more like Jesus. It's a long process. As you look back you will be able to see the progress that you have made. Failure to live as Jesus would wish is being replaced by fruitfulness in your life. You are beginning to replace anger with peace, hate with love, impatience with patience and harshness with gentleness. The ways of the world are now being replaced by what Paul calls 'the fruit of the Spirit' (Galatians 5:22–23).

The help and companionship of the Holy Spirit, the grace and the example of the Lord Jesus, and the wonderful love of God the Father have undergirded all that Paul has written to people under pressure. They are the resources he found at hand when facing his own pressures.

But does it work today? One very stressful event that held the headlines of papers and TV for weeks in 1990 was the riot in Manchester's Strangeways Prison. The senior chaplain there is Noel Proctor. He recently wrote about the way in which the love of God, and the grace of Jesus can change people under pressure:

> 'Many of the 600 plus letters we received from Christians, assuring us of their prayer support, talked of God scattering his children from Strangeways as missionaries. I doubted this, until one chaplain told me he had visited a police container unit when one officer said he had always questioned the work of prison chaplains until the lads arrived from Strangeways. A number of them read from their Bibles. Their behaviour was quite different from the rest. Quite openly they told of how they had found Jesus at Strangeways and how his power had changed them.
>
> One policeman rang me from Leamington Spa to tell me how a lad from Manchester had arrived at his station. This lad cleaned off the graffiti and dirt in his cell and then asked for paint to decorate it. Jesus had come into his life and given him a new motivation. The officer told me, "I never thought a prisoner would make me think seriously about my life!" '
>
> (Noel Proctor, 'Out of the Ashes', *Renewal* magazine, June 1991)

No matter *what* our situation, the love of God, the grace of Jesus and the friendship of the Spirit really can help us when we are under pressure. What's more, the pressures may not lessen, but the help gets greater! Once we have found the reality of God's help in our lives, we shall be able to live as Christians who may not be free from pressure but who are set free to press on.

OTHER BOOKS IN THIS SERIES

Pioneers or Settlers? Exodus: Adventurous faith for today (Philip Mohabir)

God of New Beginnings: Matthew 1–4 in today's world (Roger Sainsbury)

Thirsty for God: Matthew 5–7: Jesus' teaching for today (Stephen Gaukroger)

Drawing Power: Living out Acts in today's world (Derek Prime)

Open to Others: Ephesians: Overcoming barriers in today's church (Colin Buchanan)

Growing your Gifts: 2 Timothy: Ministry in today's world (Stephen Gaukroger)